THE
ORVIS®
— GUIDE TO —
BEGINNING FLY TYING

THE ORVIS

— GUIDE TO —

BEGINNING FLY TYING

101 TIPS for the Absolute Beginner

Preface by
TOM ROSENBAUER

David Klausmeyer

Skyhorse Publishing

Skyhorse Publishing books may be purchased in bulk at special discounts for sales promotion, corporate gifts, fund-raising, or educational purposes. Special editions can also be created to specifications. For details, contact the Special Sales Department, Skyhorse Publishing, 307 West 36th Street, 11th Floor, New York, NY 10018 or info@skyhorsepublishing.com.

Skyhorse® and Skyhorse Publishing® are registered trademarks of Skyhorse Publishing, Inc.®, a Delaware corporation.

Visit our website at www.skyhorsepublishing.com.

10 9 8 7 6 5

Library of Congress Cataloging-in-Publication Data is available on file.
ISBN: 978-1-61608-622-0

Printed in China

For fly fishers who are ready to take the next step and become fly tiers.

THE

ORVIS®

— GUIDE TO —

BEGINNING FLY TYING

Contents

Preface

WHEN WE DECIDED THERE WAS A NEED FOR A 101 TIPS BOOK on fly tying, the list of possible authors was very short, and Dave Klausmeyer was at the top. I've known Dave for about twenty years, and have watched him grow from a fly-fishing historian and bamboo rod maker to a superb editor, teacher, and photographer. And having Dave slaving by himself on some arcane bit of history or planning strips of cane in his basement is a waste of his greatest talent, which is his gregarious, open, and sympathetic manner whenever he meets a fellow fly tier. He's always happy, typically hilarious, and constantly has his ear open to what's new.

All of those talents come through in this book. From the very first entry about washing your hands and its reference to what your mother always told you, Dave endears himself to us with his openness and easy-to-read style. He has also never forgotten what it's like to be a novice fly tier with burning questions that have to be answered *right now* because you have thread hanging from a size 16 half-finished Parachute Adams and you don't know how to make a parachute post. Yeah, you could sort through all the videos on YouTube and then get sidetracked on watching a talking dog video or a clip on fly fishing for Dorado—meanwhile your Parachute Adams hangs unfinished. Wouldn't it be easier to just open a tightly organized book and find just what you are looking for, from a guy who has been at it for more years than you've been alive, as opposed to some bozo on YouTube who may have begun tying last week?

I've written a couple of fly tying books myself, and looking through these chapters I can't believe I have never mentioned stuff like thinking ahead to the next step, how to store your flies, how to read a pattern description, or whether natural fly tying materials are safe to handle. Dave has listened to novice fly tiers, carefully, and has really answered questions that both novices and experienced hands ask all the time.

I know he has answered these questions because I do a weekly podcast on fly fishing, and all of the topics I cover are suggestions from listeners. I have kept track of all the questions about fly tying I've been asked in more than 120 podcasts, and I was truly floored to find out that Dave has answered every one.

I know this book will be a treasured guide, but I also know it will make you chuckle. Who else would do a chapter called "The Craziest Fly Ever?" and then proceed to tell us about a fly tied out of a condom? Only Dave, who knows full well that fly fishing and fly tying are supposed to be fun, not deadly serious, and that fun should extend to the way we learn new stuff.

—Tom Rosenbauer
March 2012

Introduction: Enjoy the Odyssey

CHANCES ARE YOU FLY FISH. HOW DO I KNOW THIS? BECAUSE you purchased or have been given a book about how to tie flies. Sure, there are a few folks who tie but have no keen interest in fishing; they tie simply for the joy of crafting beautiful flies. These fly tiers, however, are in the minority. For the vast majority of us, learning to make flies is the next step in our odyssey to become more complete anglers.

For novice tiers, making flies that catch fish seems like alchemy. We lash bits of feathers and fur to pieces of bent wire to trick wild, scaly creatures into thinking we are giving them something good to eat. If that doesn't sound like turning lead into gold, then I don't know what does. But fly tying is not alchemy: if you have the interest, you can learn how to make your own flies that catch fish.

My goal is to take some of the mystery out of fly tying—to make it seem less like alchemy and more like a craft that you can enjoy and perhaps even master. We will deal with the most elemental basics of fly tying: how to read a pattern recipe, the three attributes of a good fly, and even how to store the flies you tie. We will discuss how to select a quality yet affordable fly-tying vise, and how to set up your fly-tying station to reduce back, neck, and eye strain. We will study the basic types of materials you will need to get started, and I will show you how to save money tying your own flies. Next, we will see how to craft the basic types of flies you will want to add to your fishing kit, and I will even challenge you to develop some of your own unique patterns. You might just create the next "hot" fly!

There's an expression in fly fishing called "time on the water." It means that your knowledge and ability to fish grows in direct proportion to how much time you spend on the river, lake, or shore with a fly rod in hand. You are the pupil, the water is the classroom, and the fish are the teachers. You'll never graduate if you don't spend sufficient time in school.

This same principle is true for learning to tie flies. Nothing replaces "time at the vise" for developing your fly-tying skills: learning to master thread control, selecting and manipulating materials, and crafting durable flies that do not easily fall apart. Any expert can demonstrate the finer points of fly tying, but how quickly you develop your skills is directly related to how much time you spend at the vise. How much time? This depends upon your schedule and how much free time you can devote to the craft, but there is a similarity between learning to tie flies and learning to play the piano: you will get more out of practicing one hour per day for five days than playing five hours before going to your next music lesson. Tie flies when time permits—even if it's only 30 or 45 minutes per session—but tie regularly, and you will develop the skills to make the patterns necessary to catch fish on your local waters.

You're already a fly fisher. Now you're ready to take the next step and become a fly tier. In short order, you will be catching fish with the very flies you tie. Enjoy the odyssey!

David Klausmeyer
First day of Spring, 2012

CHAPTER

1

First Things First: What You Need to Know to Start Tying Flies

1

Wash Your Hands

YOUR MOTHER TOLD YOU TO WASH YOUR HANDS BEFORE eating, and you should wash them before tying flies, too. Having hands free of dirt and natural oils is especially important when using light-colored materials. Grime and oil are easily transferred to tying materials, and nothing spoils the appearance of a nice fly more than soiled ingredients. It is especially easy to discolor light-colored flosses and threads.

When you're finished tying, wash your hands once again. Use plenty of soap and hot water to remove any dyes, preservatives, and other chemical agents that get transferred from the materials to your hands while tying.

Don't Crowd the Hook Eye

RUNNING OUT OF SPACE ON THE HOOK SHANK SO YOU can't make a nice thread head and tie off the fly is one of the most common fly-tying mistakes. All beginners experience this problem, and even advanced tiers occasionally run out of room before they're able to complete the fly. Here's a simple way to avoid crowding the eye of the hook.

Tie the head of the fly on the bare piece of shank behind the hook eye.

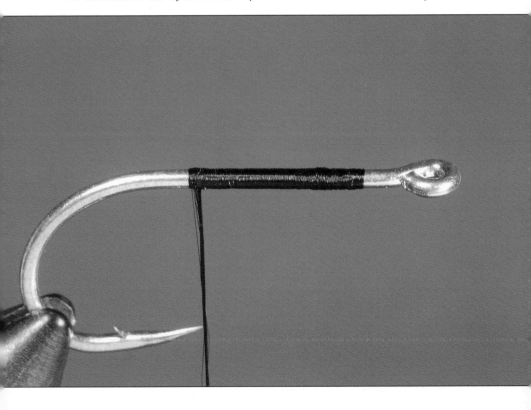

The size of the thread head is typically equal to the width of the hook eye—maybe a little larger. When beginning the fly, start the thread down the shank a distance equal to the width of the eye. This first thread wrap is a marker; don't tie any materials on the hook between this spot and the hook eye. When you're ready to complete the fly, wrap the thread head on the bare length of shank behind the hook eye.

3

Think Ahead to the Next Step

FLY TIERS AND CHESS PLAYERS HAVE SOMETHING IN COM-mon: A chess master thinks several moves ahead when playing a game, and a good tier thinks several steps ahead when dressing a fly.

The legendary Warren Duncan tied this Blue Charm salmon fly. Warren planned ahead and carefully allowed ample room to make the various parts of the body.

When tying a material to the hook, think about the next ingredient you will apply and how you will use it. Leave the thread hanging at the best position to add the next material. Be sure to leave ample room to add each material required to tie the pattern. And don't make a lot of needless and extra wraps of thread when tying on each ingredient; excess thread wraps create bulk and do not add to the strength of the fly.

As you gain skill and begin tying more complex flies, you will have to plan further ahead. Mentally divide the hook into the sections that will hold the tail, the body, and the front of the fly. Do not allow one section of the fly to encroach on the space required to make another part of the pattern.

Dick Talleur made these outstanding classic wet flies. he carefully planned each step when tying them.

4

Start with Flies You Know Will Catch Fish

"WHAT FLIES SHOULD I LEARN TO TIE FIRST?"

All beginning tiers ask this question. It is important to learn to make flies you know will maximize your odds at catching fish to increase your confidence both as an angler and a tier.

The classic March Brown is just the sort of fly that catches trout in May and June.

Inquire at your local fly shop or fishing club about the three to five best patterns that catch fish in your local waters. Tell the shop owner or club members that you are a beginning tier, and that you do not want overly complicated patterns—just solid, easy-to-tie flies that catch fish. Buy only the materials you will need to tie those flies; you'll probably discover that you can use the same thread, hooks, and other ingredients to make more than one of the patterns. It's also likely that the fly shop attendant or a club member will offer some valuable pointers or even a fly-tying lesson.

Gain confidence tying and catching fish with those basic flies, and gradually add new patterns to your fly-tying repertoire as you gain experience.

The Bi-visible is an example of a dry fly that catches trout almost everywhere.

5

Develop Consistency in the Appearance of Your Flies

YOU CAN ALWAYS TELL FLIES DRESSED BY AN ACCOMPLISHED tier: They have the same proportions and style. And you can always spot the patterns of a neophyte: They're a hodgepodge of sizes, shapes, and proportions. It's easy to understand how an experienced tier can make ten of the same pattern all look pretty much alike, but even when he changes patterns—say, from tying a Royal Coachman to a Quill Gordon—he uses the same sense of proportions in the tails, wings, and hackle. When the novice

All these dainty dry flies were obviously made by the same fly dresser.

makes ten of the same fly, however, they often look as though they came from ten completely different tiers; the tails, bodies, wings, and hackles are all different sizes and tied with very different proportions.

Pay close attention to the proportions you use when tying a fly. And be mindful of the height of the wings, the length of the tails, the width of the hackle collars, and so on. Don't hop around tying different patterns; tie ten of the same fly to develop a sense of size and proportion. Before you know it, the contents of your fly box will look like a polished army ready for inspection and to do battle with the fish.

The author tied these imitations of a golden stonefly nymph. They all look very similar.

6

The Three Attributes of a Good Fly

WHAT MAKES A GOOD FISH-CATCHING FLY? THIS IS ONE OF the most debated questions in the sport of fly fishing. And as a fly tier, this question will always be on your mind: Will the fly I am tying really catch a fish?

Scientists have determined that fish have a poor ability to detect details in the objects around them, so adding lots of extra features to our flies to

The Crystal Bugger is a great trout and bass pattern. The bright body attracts the attention of the fish, and the wavy marabou tail makes the fly look alive in the water.

precisely match the appearance of real food probably makes little difference. Fish react—feed, flee, mate, and more—out of instinct and impulse; they do not have the brainpower to make thoughtful, reasoned decisions. This is why they ignore the hooks and tippets hanging off our flies.

The best flies match three basic characteristics that fish are looking for in the food they eat: size, shape, and natural-looking movement. A good fly matches the general size of a real food item: an insect, baitfish, or perhaps some form of crustacean. A quality fly should also match the general shape of real food. And finally, the fly should imitate the movement—or lack of motion—of real food.

The color of the fly is less important than the size, shape, and action of the pattern. An olive or black Woolly Bugger, for example, is a known fish-catcher; the soft, marabou tail has a natural swimming action that few fish can resist.

7

How to Read a Fly Pattern Recipe

TYING A FLY IS A LOT LIKE BAKING A CAKE: YOU MAKE BOTH using a variety of ingredients. A fly recipe is very similar to a cake recipe in that it lists everything you need to make the pattern: the hook, thread, feathers, furs, and all of the other materials. Check out the following recipe for the classic Fan-wing Royal Coachman dry fly; it lists everything you will need to tie it.

The first ingredient is the hook; place this in the vise when you start the fly. Next comes the thread; the first tying procedure is to wrap some thread

on the hook shank. The remainder of the materials are listed in the order in which you will tie them to the hook.

Hook: Light-wire, dry-fly hook, size 16 to 12.
Thread: Brown 8/0 (70 denier).
Tail: Golden-pheasant, tippet fibers.
Body: Peacock herl and red floss.
Wing: White-hen, chicken hackle tips.
Hackle: Brown.

8

Will I Save Money Tying My Own Flies?

WHETHER OR NOT YOU SAVE MONEY TYING YOUR OWN flies depends upon how many you make. First, if you tie a lot of different patterns, and are always adding more to your repertoire, you probably will not save money; tying a great variety of flies requires buying many more materials, which increases the expense of tying. On the other hand, if you specialize in making a few choice patterns that catch fish on your local waters, and you fish and tie a lot, you might break even and perhaps even save a little money making your own flies.

Tying flies in order to save money is probably a mistake. Instead, think of fly tying as a wonderful extension of your fishing; it gives you an opportunity to enjoy the sport when you are not on the water, and you will discover the added thrill of catching fish with your very own flies. In fact, many tiers in northern climates consider winter as "fly-tying season."

9

Should I Buy a Fly-Tying Kit or Individual Materials?

A FLY-TYING KIT IS A WONDERFUL CHRISTMAS OR birthday present for a fledgling fly fisher; it will open that person's eyes to the possibilities of making his or her own flies. If you already own a fly-tying kit, congratulations: You're about to embark on a wonderful new hobby!

The Orvis Clearwater Fly-Tying Kit is a fine starting pointing for new tiers.

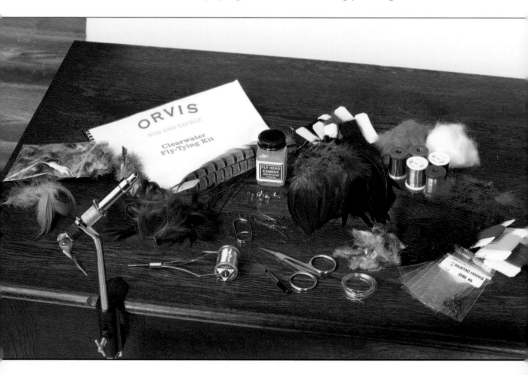

A fly-tying kit might not be the best choice for someone who has decided to take up tying and plans to make a lot of his own patterns. It's hard for a manufacturer to assemble a kit that contains only the tools and materials every tier will use, so it might contain some things that will be of no use to you. A kit offered by a leading company in the fly-fishing industry, however, will contain a more useful variety of tools and materials.

Selecting a fly-tying kit or purchasing tools and materials a la carte depends upon your level of interest and goals. If you just want to dabble and test your interest in the craft, a quality kit is a fine starting point; If you are determined to tie a lot of flies and are willing to do the research about what you will need to get started, then buy individual tools and materials.

Another example of a fine fly-tying kit offered by the Orvis Company.

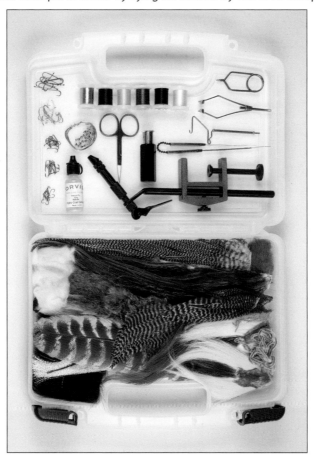

10

Where Can I Learn More about Fly Tying?

WHILE IT USED TO BE DIFFICULT TO FIND INFORMATION on tying flies, such is no longer the case. Today we have a variety of great sources for learning how to tie.

Almost all fly shops and fly-fishing clubs offer fly-tying classes; some conduct classes on an on-going basis, and most of these sessions are free or cost very little. Many adult education programs also offer fine fly-tying classes; If your local adult-ed program does not offer a class, call and request that they start one. Your local bookstore or library will probably have a shelf or two featuring fly-tying books, and there are instructional DVDs and videos that teach everything from beginning to the more advanced forms of fly tying. There are also dozens of websites containing homemade fly-tying videos; Some of this content is of low quality, but a great deal of it is actually very good and useful. And last but not least, *Fly Tyer* magazine, which is the world's largest magazine devoted to art of tying flies, contains articles that appeal to both novice and experienced tiers.

Fly fishing and tying have a great literary tradition. These two classic volumes offer much wisdom to modern fly tiers.

How Should I Store My Flies?

YOU'VE WORKED HARD TO TIE YOUR FLIES; NOW YOU must assure that they'll remain in good condition for when you go fishing. Properly stored, a fly will last many years.

Always select a fly box designed to accommodate the type of flies you tie. A box made to store saltwater patterns is larger and can hold bigger flies, and a box designed for freshwater streamers is longer so the flies can lay flat and not become permanently bent during storage. Larger boxes also contain ample space to allow air to circulate between the flies to keep them dry.

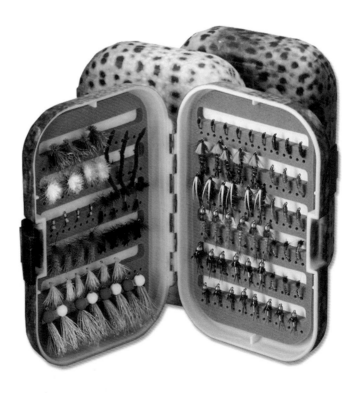

Dry-fly, wet-fly, and nymph boxes are generally smaller and easily fit in a vest pocket. Many boxes have small individual compartments; These are particularly good for housing dry flies so the fine hackle collars do not become bent. Many fly boxes have foam ridges to hold nymphs and larvae patterns; simply stick the hooks into the foam to secure the flies in place. The best fly boxes have watertight seals to keep their insides dry if they fall into the water.

Always open your fly box after fishing to allow the contents to dry. Just a couple of moist flies can raise the humidity inside a closed fly box and cause hooks to rust. Place a desiccant pack inside the box to absorb moisture and keep your flies dry.

Basic Terminology: What Is a Nymph, Larva, Emerger, and Dry Fly?

BEFORE WE CAN TALK ABOUT TROUT FLIES, WE MUST establish a common language describing the different patterns we will tie. Although some tiers split hairs and quibble about these definitions—what's

Here we see (*clockwise starting at the top*) a dry fly, a larva, an emerger, and a nymph.

a hobby without a bit of good-natured quibbling—any experienced angler will understand these terms.

A *nymph* is generally an immature stonefly, mayfly, damselfly, dragonfly, or other insect living along a streambed or lakebed. Almost all of these insects spend the majority of their lives under the water and emerge to reproduce. We tie a nymph to imitate one of these forms of trout food.

A *larva* is generally an immature caddisfly living along the streambed or lakebed.

(Important note: Nymphs and larvae constitute the bulk of a trout's diet.)

An *emerger* is the stage of an insect swimming or crawling to the surface to turn into a winged adult.

A *dry fly* is an imitation of an adult insect. A dry fly is designed to float on the surface of the water. Use a dry fly when the trout are visibly eating adult insects from the surface.

13

What Is the Best-Selling Fly In the World?

DO YOU WANT TO KNOW WHAT CATCHES FISH? HOW ABOUT what to tie? Perhaps we can answer these questions by seeing what flies anglers are buying.

According to Umpqua Feather Merchants, which is the leading commercial fly-tying outfit, the Copper John is the best-selling fly in the world.

Colorado's John Barr created the Copper John. His pattern displays many of the most modern features used to tie small nymphs: a bead head, a copper wire body, and a dab of epoxy on the wing case. The success of the Copper John led other fly designers to include these components in many of their patterns.

With the introduction of Ultra Wire, which is copper wire anodized in a wide variety of colors, the Copper John is now dressed in yellow, olive, green, blue, and many other colors. While he does not know the reason, Barr says that a red Copper John catches more fish than any other variety of his famous fly.

There are many variations of the common Copper John. Here we see a rubber-legged version.

14

Commemorative Flies Are Fun to Tie

AS YOUR FLY-TYING SKILLS DEVELOP, YOU MAY WISH TO create flies for family and friends. You can tie a new fly to commemorate an important event, or you can name a fly for a cherished person in your life. Tying these sorts of flies is fun, and the people who receive them are thrilled.

Charlie Mann, of Maine, is a lifelong outdoorsman and supporter of the Maine Warden Service. Charlie has named many of his classically inspired streamers for game wardens and others who make Maine an important destination for anglers and hunters. Here we see his commemorative fly called the Maine Guide. Charlie designed this lovely streamer using the colors found in the shoulder patch awarded to the skilled outdoorsmen and women who earn the rank of Registered Maine Guide.

Have fun and create your own original patterns. Give them to friends and family, and watch their faces light up!

CHAPTER

2

Choosing and Using the Right Tools

15

What Is a Fly-Tying Vise?

THE VISE IS THE TOOL THAT HOLDS THE HOOK AND ALLOWS you tie on the furs, feathers, and other materials. The head of the vise holds the jaws and the jaws' locking mechanism. The head, in turn, is attached to a stem and some sort of clamp or heavy pedestal base. This is the original style of fly-tying vise, and many excellent examples are still manufactured. Select one of these vises only if you have no interest in learning rotary fly-tying techniques.

The Dyna-King Kingfisher is a high-quality entry-level vise that will last a lifetime.

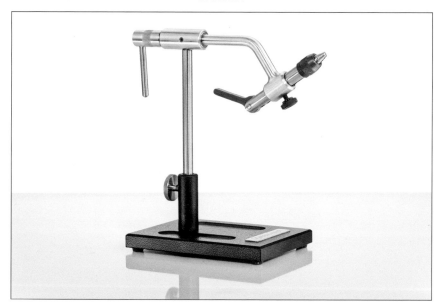

The head on a rotary vise easily turns the hook so you can apply materials while spinning the hook. Even if you do not use rotary fly-tying techniques, a rotary vise lets you easily turn the hook so that you can inspect all sides of a fly.

Go to a quality fly shop and ask the proprietor to show you the features and benefits of the different vises he carries. Ask him to demonstrate using the vises in your price range.

16

How to Select a Vise

THE VISE WILL PROBABLY BE YOUR LARGEST SINGLE expense when getting into fly tying, but a quality vise will offer a lifetime of service and enjoyment. You will use your vise to tie all of your flies. As a result, you will want to carefully consider which vise you purchase. Consider these questions when choosing a vise.

- Will the vise accommodate all of the sizes of hooks I plan to use? Clamp the smallest and largest hook in the vise to see if they fit.

The HMH Spartan accommodates other jaws and a variety of accessories. ▶

- Will this vise hold a hook securely without applying a great deal of force to close the jaws?
- Do I have to spend a lot of time adjusting the vise to get the jaws to hold the hook properly? (You want to spend your time tying flies, not fidgeting with your tools.)
- Does the vise offer sufficient working room between the hook and bench top? Can I adjust the vise to get more working room?
- Does the vise come with accessories such as a bobbin rest and materials clip (used to conveniently hold tinsel and similar materials out of the way while tying other parts of a fly)?
- Does the vise come with a good warranty?

If you plan to tie midges and other tiny flies, make sure your new vise can accommodate the small hooks.

17

Do You Need a Vise with a C-Clamp or a Pedestal Vise?

WHEN SELECTING A VISE, ONE OF THE FIRST DECISIONS you will have to make is whether to buy one with a c-clamp or heavy pedestal base. A c-clamp locks the vise to the table or tying bench, and is therefore the most secure type of vise. You can place a vise mounted on a pedestal on any table, bench, or even a lapboard, so it is very portable. When choosing between a c-clamp or pedestal vise, consider the type of flies you plan to make and where you plan to tie.

Tying a deer-hair bass bug requires placing a lot of tension on the thread and hook. Most tiers who specialize in making bass bugs prefer using vises with c-clamps so the fly remains stationary when tension is applied to the thread. With a c-clamp, however, you are limited to using only tables and benches that will accept the size of the clamp you are using. As a result, these vises are not very portable; I have taught many fly-tying classes where students arrived with c-clamp vises that did not fit the tables that were provided.

Pedestal vises are portable and perfectly acceptable for tying the majority of flies; thread used to tie the average trout fly, for example, will snap before the vise moves on the table. And, of course, you can move the vise out of the way when preparing or counting out materials, and move it back into position when you're ready to tie. Just be sure to select a pedestal vise with a heavy base; Avoid any pedestal made of aluminum or some other light-weight material.

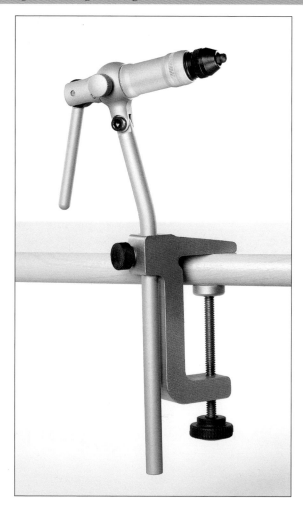

The Renzetti Apprentice is an example of ▶ a vise with a c-clamp base.

18

What Is Rotary Fly Tying?

MOST PEOPLE THINK THAT YOU TIE A FLY BY PLACING A hook in a fixed vise, and your right hand (assuming you are right-handed) wraps the thread and other materials onto the hook shank. This is the traditional way of tying a fly. With rotary fly tying, however, the opposite occurs: The head of the vise and hook rotate while your hands remain stationary, holding the materials. As if by magic, the ingredients wrap onto the shank as the hook spins.

Check out the example of wrapping a tinsel rib in the accompanying photographs. I placed the hook in the vise so it will spin, with the shank acting as the axis of the turning hook. The rib neatly wraps on the hook as

1. Start tying the fly: tie on a piece of tinsel and wrap the floss body. Hang the thread on the bobbin rest.

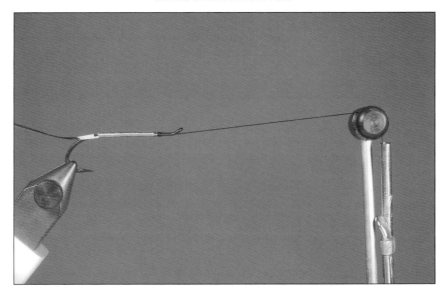

I turn the vise. This method works for applying most ingredients that are wrapped on the hook shank: thread, floss, tinsel, wire, dubbing, and many braided materials.

Rotary fly tying is a favorite technique of commercial fly tiers interested in increasing their production.

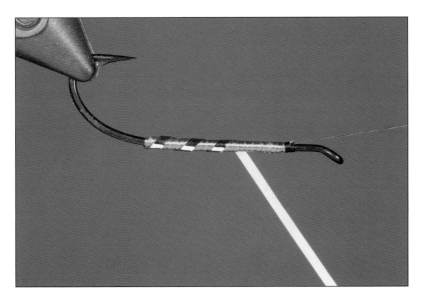

2. Turn the head and jaws on the rotary vise; The tinsel neatly wraps up the body.

3. Tie off and clip the excess piece of tinsel.

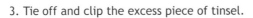

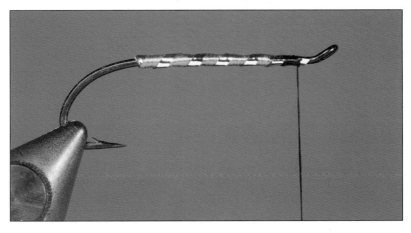

19

The Proper Way to Place a Hook in the Vise

MANY BEGINNING FLY TIERS ARE SURPRISED TO LEARN that there is a correct—and an incorrect—way to mount a hook in the vise.

Some manufacturers report receiving returned vises that have tiny chips in the tips of the jaws. Fly tiers see photographs of flies perched in the very ends of the jaws, and believe this is the proper way to clamp a hook in a vise. In truth, very little clamping pressure is needed when you're taking a photograph; When tying a fly, however, you have to apply more pressure to

This fly is perched in the tip of the jaws. This is the wrong way to mount a hook in the vise.

tightly clamp the hook in place. As a result of this increased force, the tips of even the best vises might chip.

When clamping a hook in the vise, place the hook deep into the jaws to maximize the amount of surface contact between the inside of the jaws and the hook; this will reduce the amount of pressure you will have to apply to get the hook to hold still while tying the fly. Position the hook shank level or cocked slightly upright; do not place the shank angling downward or the thread will slip off the front when completing the fly.

This is the correct way to place a hook in a vise; The jaws can clamp the hook without applying excessive pressure on the locking mechanism.

How to Maintain a Vise

A QUALITY VISE REQUIRES VERY LITTLE MAINTENANCE. But, even the best vises—made of the finest materials—will eventually show small amounts of fine rust, especially on the jaws.

If you detect rust on your vise's jaws, remove it using grade 0000 steel wool. Lightly buff the metal to remove the rust. NEVER use a coarser grade of steel wool or apply too much pressure, as this can scratch the surface of your vise. Every few months, lightly spray the metal surfaces of the vise with fine oil. Use a clean cloth to wipe away any excess oil.

Apply one tiny drop of fine oil to every pivot point and joint on the head and stem of the vise. Wipe away any excess with a clean cloth.

Always remove the last hook from the vise jaws when you complete your tying session. Never leave a hook clamped in the vise with the idea that you will return later to complete the fly; Relieve the tension on the vise to avoid fatiguing the jaws or locking mechanism.

Remove the last hook when you're done tying. Release
the tension on the jaws and locking mechanism.

21

What Other Fly-Tying Tools Do I Need?

GOING TO A SPECIALTY STORE AND ASKING "WHAT DO I need" is a dangerous question: An unscrupulous or unknowledgeable proprietor might load you down will all sorts of gadgets that will not meet your needs. This short list of small tools is all you will need to start tying flies.

- A quality bobbin holds spooled materials such as thread and floss while you tie a fly.
- A bodkin, which is a heavy needle with a handle, is excellent for picking hairs and other fibers off of a fly, applying cement to the thread head of a finished pattern, and numerous other uses.
- A hair stacker evens the tips of a bunch of hair when tying the wing on an Elk-hair Caddis and similar flies.
- High-quality scissors. You can skimp on expenses in some areas, but purchase the best scissors you can afford.
- Hackle pliers grasp the tip of a hackle while you wrap the feather on the fly.

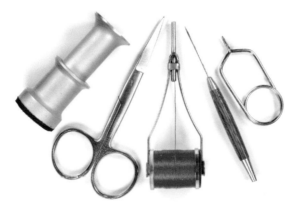

A Backing Plate Reduces Eye Strain

A BACKING PLATE IS A DEVICE THAT SETS BEHIND THE VISE and contrasts with the color of the pattern you are tying, making it easier to see the fly and reducing eyestrain. For example, tying a brown fly against a dark wooden tabletop is difficult; a background of a different color makes it much easier to see your work.

Commercial backing plates are available for most vises, but anything that contrasts with the color of the fly you are tying will work; even a sheet of paper will make it easier to see the fly.

You can purchase a backing plate to fit the stems of most vises, but you can also use a sheet of paper or anything that provides contrast to the color of the fly you are tying.

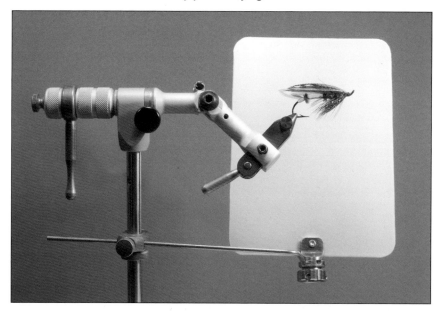

23

Select the Correct Scissors for the Job

QUALITY SCISSORS WILL CUT ALMOST ANY FLY-TYING material, but many are designed for specific applications. For example, use scissors with fine tips, lightweight handles, and small serrations to trim natural materials such as hair, fur, and feathers. If you plan to tie deer-hair bass bugs, select scissors with thicker serrations in one blade: The serrations hold the hair fibers while the sharp, non-serrated blade does the actual cutting.

Synthetic materials are especially tough on fine scissors and will quickly dull the blades. If you plan to use a lot of synthetic hair and flash materials, buy scissors specified for use with these types of ingredients. The blades will

Bass-bug guru Chris Helm crafted this great mouse using deer hair. Scissors designed to clip deer hair make the job much easier.

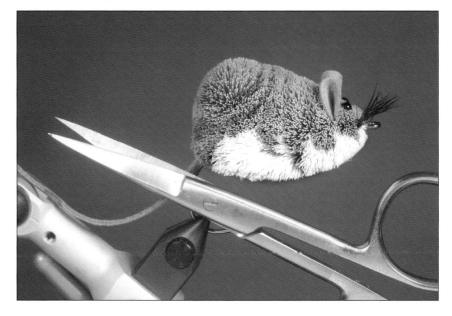

be a little heavier and probably made of carbon steel so they can hold an edge longer.

Never use fine-tipped or lightweight fly-tying scissors to cut wire or other metals. These materials will quickly dull the blades and loosen the screw or rivet holding the blades together. Either use scissors marketed for use with these materials, or purchase an inexpensive pair of scissors that you replace when the blades become dull and unusable.

Fly-tying expert Pat Cohen crafted this amazing fish using spun deer hair.

24

Proper Bobbin Technique for Improved Thread Wrapping

YOU'VE MOUNTED A SPOOL OF THREAD IN YOUR BOBBIN, and started the thread on the hook: Great, you're ready to tie a fly! But, did you know that there are simple techniques that will make it much easier to use and control your bobbin?

First, grasp the narrow bobbin tube between your thumb and forefinger, and place the spool of thread and body of the bobbin in the palm of your hand. The ends of your fingers should be near the tip of the tube. This will give you the best grip on the bobbin and increase your control over the tool.

Second, only a short piece of thread should extend between the tip of the bobbin and the hook. Using the smallest amount of thread will increase your ability to control the tension and accurately place thread wraps on the hook.

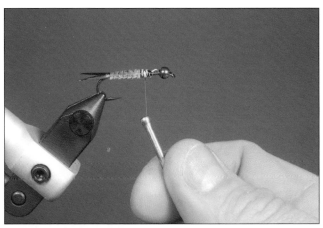

25

Off-Hand Tying Techniques

HOW YOU HOLD THE BOBBIN AND USE YOUR DOMINANT tying hand is important to your ability to efficiently tie nice flies. How you use your non-dominant off hand is equally important to developing correct fly-tying skills.

You'll typically hold materials on the hook using your off hand while wrapping the thread and tying them to the fly using your dominant hand. Carefully and accurately position the materials on the hook. Grasp the materials as close as possible to the hook so they remain in place and do not roll around the shank when applying thread pressure; Avoid holding your fingers far from the hook when applying new materials to the shank.

1. Grasp the end of the material near the tips of your fingers. Place the material in position on the hook. Tie the material in place.

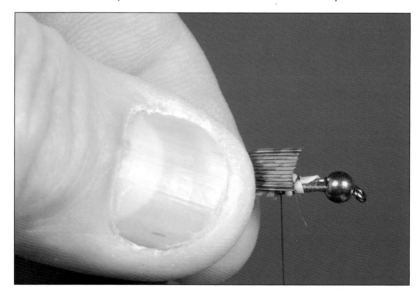

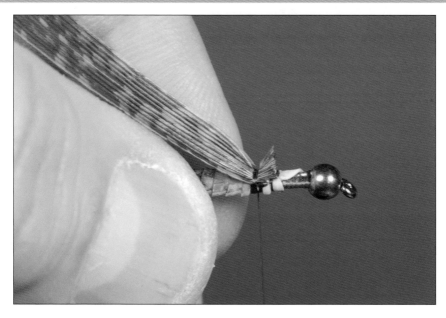

2. Always avoid holding your fingers far from the hook when applying new materials to the shank.

26

The Half-Hitch Is a Very Important Knot

THE HALF-HITCH IS AN ESSENTIAL KNOT FOR TYING NEAT flies: it is a snap to make, it does a fine job of holding things in place between steps, and it adds no bulk. In fact, rather than making a complicated whip-finish to complete the head of a fly before snipping the thread, just make three or four half-hitches and add a drop of cement. I've used this method of finishing flies for more than thirty years, and my patterns never fall apart.

Stop struggling to learn how to use a whip-finishing tool. Instead, learn how to make a simple half-hitch. With practice, you can place a half-hitch exactly where you wish on the hook.

1. Extend about four inches of thread from the tip of the bobbin. Hold the bobbin in your off hand. Place the tips of your forefinger and index finger against the thread.

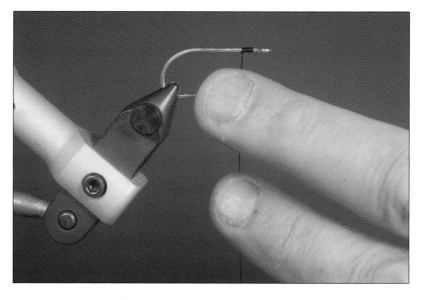

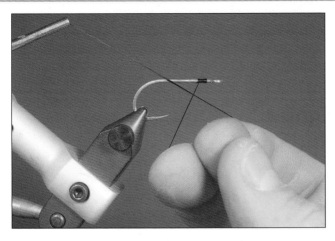

2. Raise the bobbin to the left and turn your fingers so the thread crosses.

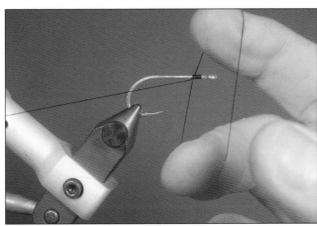

3. Place the loop of thread on the hook.

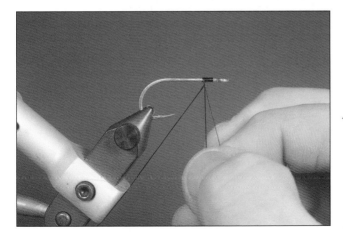

4. Pinch the loop of thread between your index and forefinger. Start drawing the bobbin and thread to the left to close the loop.

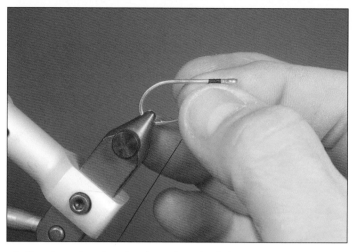

5. Continue drawing the thread to the left to completely close the loop of thread on the hook. Continue grasping the loop until the knot tightens.

6. Our half-hitch knot is done. With a little practice, you can place a half-hitch anywhere you wish on the hook.

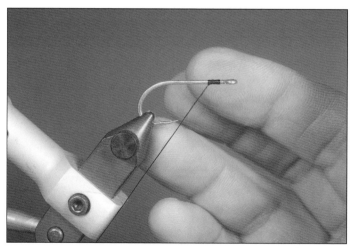

27

Which Bobbin Should I Use?

OUR GOAL IS TO DEMYSTIFY FLY TYING AND MAKE IT EASY and accessible. However, just like with selecting the correct scissors to do a job, it helps to understand the different types of bobbins and choose the one that best meets your needs.

A bobbin is a simple tool that holds spooled materials, typically thread or floss. The bobbin makes it easy to grasp the spool while tying a fly, and it allows you to let the spool hang from the fly without unraveling. You'll find a selection of bobbins in the fly-tying section of any fly shop.

Here we see the tips (*left to right*) of a plain metal-tubed bobbin, a ceramic bobbin, and a floss bobbin.

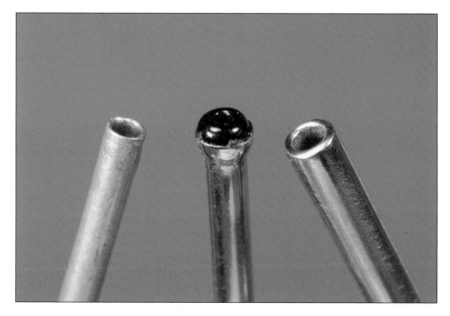

First, you'll need a bobbin to hold spools of thread. This sort of bobbin will have a narrow metal tube made of metal or hard plastic. Sometimes the tip of a metal tube has a ceramic insert to prevent the thread from contacting the edge of the metal tube and fraying; this tool is called a "ceramic bobbin." A ceramic bobbin costs a couple of dollars more than a plain metal-tubed bobbin, but it is typically worth the slight extra expense.

If you plan to tie flies requiring floss bodies, such as classic wet flies, streamers, and salmon or steelhead flies, you will want a floss bobbin. A floss bobbin has a wider tube to accommodate this thicker material. While you can simply clip a length of floss off the spool, tie it to the hook, and then wrap the body of the fly, placing the spool in a bobbin keeps the floss cleaner and you will waste less material.

In addition to the bobbin, a bobbin threader is a convenient tool for getting the thread or floss through the narrow tube. You can purchase an actual bobbin threader at your neighborhood fly shop, but a looped piece of monofilament will also serve as a simple and inexpensive threader.

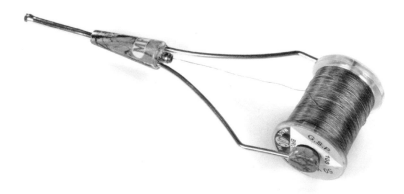

Set Your Chair and Vise at the Proper Height

SELECT YOUR CHAIR AND TYING WORKBENCH OR TABLE carefully. Your chair should be comfortable and offer ample back support. Tie at a table, desk, or bench that allows you to set the vise jaws about even with your lower chest. If your arms or shoulders become fatigued, try lowering your vise; If the back of your neck becomes strained because you are humped over while you tie, raise your vise so you're looking straight at the fly.

Too many tiers complain of shoulder and neck pain. You can largely eliminate these common problems by choosing the proper chair and placing the vise in the correct position.

Select a workbench that lets you set the vise jaws about even with your lower chest. Now add a comfortable chair with good back support, and you're ready to tie. (*Courtesy of Orvis*)

◀

Feathers, Furs, and More: Selecting the Right Materials for Tying Flies

It Is Okay to Substitute Materials When Tying a Fly?

MANY FLY TIERS BELIEVE THEY MUST USE THE EXACT ingredients listed in a pattern recipe when tying a fly; they would never dream of using other brands or colors of materials. But what happens if your local fly shop doesn't have one or more of the ingredients specified in the recipe? Does this mean you can't tie the fly? Of course not.

Feel free to substitute with other materials when tying a fly. It is often possible to select a different but similar color or brand and create a close copy of the pattern. So what if your finished fly looks a bit different? It just might catch more fish.

Look at this basic Bead-Head Hare's-Ear Nymph; this is one of the first patterns you'll learn to make in fly-tying class. The original recipe calls for hare's-ear dubbing for the body, but you can substitute with standard rabbit dubbing or a wide variety of packaged natural, synthetic, and blended natural/synthetic dubbings. You can make the tail using pheasant tail fibers, hackle fibers, or almost any mottled duck flank fibers. In fact, you can tie this pattern using a regular nymph hook, a long-shank nymph hook, or even a curved-shank nymph hook. You can use an almost unlimited combination of materials to create a very similar fish-catching pattern.

30

Count Out the Materials before You Tie

ONE OF THE SIMPLEST WAYS TO INCREASE YOUR FLY-TYING speed is to count and lay out the materials you will use before making a group of flies. Let's say you want to tie a half-dozen Light Hendrickson dry flies. Lay out six size 14 dry-fly hooks, six light ginger hackles, a small bunch of Hendrickson pink dubbing for making the bodies, and several wood duck feathers for fashioning the wings. Place a spool of pink or tan thread in your bobbin. Now you're ready to tie the flies. This simple method will keep your workspace cleaner, you'll tie more efficiently, and you'll make more flies in less time.

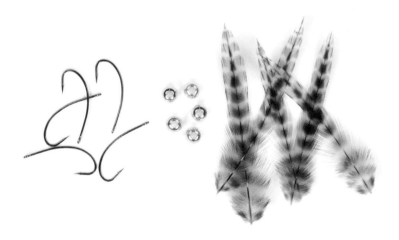

31

Simple Ideas for Storing Materials

HOW ARE YOU GOING TO STORE YOUR GROWING COLLEC-tion of fly-tying materials? An efficient storage system should serve three goals: keep your fly-tying area clean, organize your materials so you can quickly find what you need, and protect natural ingredients—hair and feath-ers—from pests. There are many wonderful fly-tying stations that are also great-looking pieces of furniture and fit well into most homes.

A tackle box is another option. A big tackle box conveniently holds large amounts of materials and is portable. Select a tackle box that has trays for

This fly-tying station, manufactured by the Oasis Company, is both efficient and looks great.

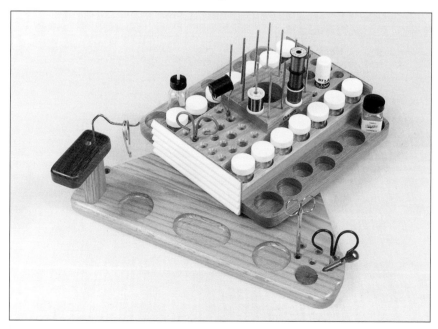

arranging small tools and spools of thread and wire, and a long, flat bottom for accommodating dry-fly hackle capes and similar bulky objects. Plastic freezer bags are ideal for organizing groups of materials; you could have separate bags containing packs of hooks, floss, dubbing, and so on. Store the bags in the tackle box, and toss in a few mothballs to ward off pests that might attack your precious materials.

This storage system is particularly ideal if you do not have space in your home or apartment to set up a permanent fly-tying station, or if you'd like to take your tying materials with you on your next fishing trip.

Deciphering Thread Sizes

THERE ARE A WIDE VARIETY OF THREAD SIZES, BUT YOU'LL only need two or three to make the majority of flies; the other sizes of thread—at the very large and extra small ends of the range—are for specialized applications. Typically, use size 3/0 for tying saltwater flies and bass bugs, size 6/0 for freshwater streamers and nymphs, and size 8/0 for trout dry flies. Note, however, that there is no industry standard for determining the diameter ratings of thread, and one manufacturer's size 6/0 might be comparable to another company's size 8/0.

Recently, some fly-tying materials suppliers adopted the "denier" thread rating system from the garment and cloth industries. This method rates the actual weight, rather than the diameter, of the thread, so you can make exact comparisons between different brands of thread.

Size 3/0 = 210 denier
Size 6/0 = 160 denier
Size 8/0 = 80 denier

33

Soft Materials Give Flies Realistic Movement

WHICH IS THE MOST IMPORTANT: TO FISH WITH A FLY THAT looks realistic, or to use one that has a realistic swimming action? As you gain more fly-fishing experience, you'll probably come to the conclusion that flies that pulsate, swim, and breathe in the water catch more fish. While it's hard to give small flies realistic swimming action, it's relatively easy to make larger patterns such as streamers appear to be alive. Using soft, flowing materials is the key.

Marabou and soft hackles pump and flow in the water. Soft hairs also make flies look alive. Some synthetic materials are a little too stiff and make flies look like swimming paint brushes, which is no surprise because some of these ingredients are used in real brushes. Soft, synthetic hairs, as well as flowing flash materials, are great for tying baitfish imitations that look alive.

Always remember to consider how a fly looks *and* behaves in the water, and that how a fly moves is often more important.

The White Marabou Muddler, featuring a white marabou wing, is one of the author's favorite trout and bass flies.

34

Protect the Environment: Use Non-Toxic Wire, Beads, and Cone Heads

AT SOME POINT YOU WILL TIE FLIES REQUIRING LEAD WIRE wrapped on the hook shank, and perhaps dumbbell eyes or bead heads. These materials add weight to the flies so they sink. They are most commonly used on freshwater nymphs and streamers, and on many saltwater baitfish imitations.

Tungsten beads, dumbbell eyes, and cove heads add weight to flies and are lead-free.

TUNGSTEN
CONEHEADS
FAST SINKING

SIZE	COLOR
☐ SMALL	☐ COPPER
☐ MEDIUM	☐ BLACK
☐ LARGE	☐ GOLD
	☐ NICKEL

Here's the rub: You will occasionally lose a fly, and you do not want to add lead to the environment. In fact, there have been proposals to eliminate the use of lead sinkers for baitfishing, much like lead shot was prohibited for hunting waterfowl many years ago.

Rather than using lead wire, beads, and dumbbells, select non-lead substitutes such as tungsten, which is heavier than lead and will quickly sink your subsurface flies to the desired depth. Brass beads are also commonly available.

This crab pattern was tied using a lead-free dumbbell.

35

What Glues Do I Need?

ALL FLY SHOPS CARRY HEAD CEMENT. DAVE'S FLEXAMENT IS a popular cement that remains slightly flexible when dry; it is ideal when you want a durable yet slightly soft and flexible finish. For most other fly-tying applications, ordinary clear fingernail polish is an ideal and commonly used cement.

Epoxy is also widely used to tie flies. Hundreds of saltwater patterns specify using epoxy to form the heads and backs of these flies; a few tiers have even developed reputations for creating patterns featuring epoxy. Avoid using five-minute epoxy; this material hardens too quickly and you'll waste more glue that you will use. Select a variety of epoxy with a longer curing time, and apply the glue to a batch of flies at one time.

Be sure to follow all the warning labels on the glues you select, and be sure to use these products with adequate ventilation.

New Jersey's Bob Popovics is famous for his Surf Candy series of saltwater baitfish imitations. The epoxy head on this Surf Candy is very durable.

What is the Difference between Dry-Fly and Hen Hackle?

HACKLES ARE THE FEATHERS THAT COME FROM THE NECKS of chickens. They are one of the most important ingredients for tying trout flies.

As the name implies, use dry-fly hackle to make flies that float. The best feathers contain lots of stiff fibers that keep flies perched on the surface film. The quills are also narrow to reduce bulk, and they do not twist when you wrap the feathers around hooks.

Use hen hackle to tie wet flies and nymphs. The softer fibers give these flies realistic swimming action that mimics insects struggling to the surface.

Fly shops sell both dry-fly and hen capes, which are the complete pelts of feathers. A quality cape contains hundreds of feathers in a wide range of sizes. You can also buy packages of hackles to tie smaller batches of flies; these offer a great way to save money and still tie with high-quality materials.

Purchase the best hackles you can afford. Nothing leads to frustration faster than tying with poor-quality hackle.

This adult drake imitation (*left*) was tied using a dry-fly hackle; the bead-head wet fly was made using a wet-fly hackle.

What Are the Different Ways to Wrap a Hackle on a Hook?

THERE ARE TWO BASIC WAYS TO WRAP A HACKLE ON A hook. Wrapping the feather around the hook behind the eye is the first common method. This creates what is called a "hackle collar," and is used to tie high-floating dry flies. A hackle collar typically consists of four or five turns of hackle around the hook, but some patterns, such as a bushy Royal Wulff, will have many more wraps.

This classic dry fly, tied by Mike Valla, has a typical hackle collar wrapped at the base of the wings.

Spiral-wrapping the hackle up the hook is the second most common method. If you take a beginner's fly-tying class, this might be the first technique you'll learn when the teacher shows you how to make a Woolly Bugger; this is often the first fly covered in tying classes.

Use fine dry-fly hackles for making floating flies. Select saddle hackle when tying Woolly Buggers and some large nymphs.

A saddle hackle spiral-wrapped up the body of this large stonefly nymph imitates the legs of the natural insect.

How to Start the Thread on the Hook

YOU'RE AT YOUR FLY-TYING STATION AND A HOOK IS IN the vise. All the materials are laid out in front of you, and the thread is your bobbin. You are ready to tie a fly! The first step is to start the thread on the hook shank. It sounds simple, yet this basic fly-tying procedure stymies many novice tiers. Here's how to start the thread on the hook.

First, grasp the bobbin in your dominant hand, and the tag end of the thread between the thumb and forefinger of your other hand; the entire length of thread should measure only about two inches. Next, place the

1. Place the thread against the hook. Hold the tag up and to the left at a 45-degree angle. (The spool of the thread and the bobbin are down and out of the photo.) Begin wrapping the spooled thread onto the tag.

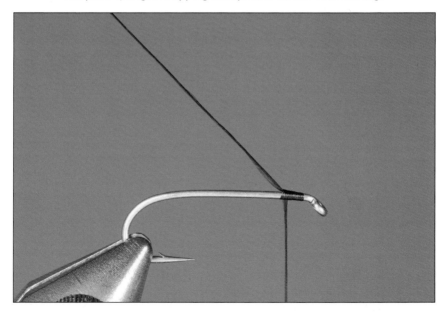

thread against the near side of the hook; most tiers position the tag end of thread above the hook shank. Hold the tag end at a 45-degree angle, and make four or five wraps onto the base of the tag. Continue holding the tag end at a 45-degree angle and wrap toward the end of the hook; each new wrap of thread will neatly slip down the tag into position on the hook. Wrap the thread all the way to the end of the shank and tie the fly.

2. Continue holding the tag end of the thread at a 45-degree angle. Wrap the spooled thread toward the end of the hook. Each new thread wrap slips down the tag and neatly into place on the hook.

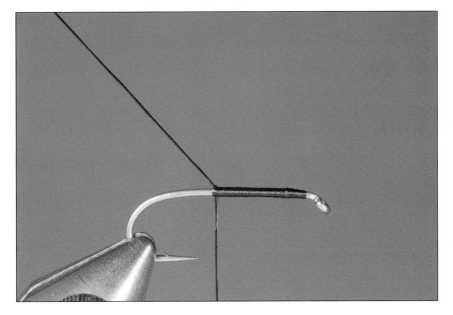

Measuring Materials Leads To Consistency

ONE OF THE HALLMARKS OF A GOOD FLY TIER IS THAT ALL of his patterns look the same; they appear as though they all popped out of the same vise. The key is maintaining similar proportions in the various parts of the flies. The length and number of fibers used to tie the tails are roughly the same. The diameter of the bodies is the same. The size and proportions of the wings are the same, and a careful tier uses the same number of wraps to make the hackle collar. Whether he is dressing dry flies, nymphs, streamers, saltwater patterns, or bass bugs, he plans ahead so each component looks the same.

The hook is a very convenient measuring device for judging the length and proportions of the parts of the flies you tie. The overall length of the shank, width of the gap, and the length from the hook point to the tip of the barb are just a few of the dimensions you can use for measuring materials. When you change hook sizes, the sizes of these dimensions will change accordingly; whether you are tying a size 22 or size 12 fly, the proportions remain consistent.

Use the hook to measure the dimensions of the different pats of a fly. For example, the length of the hook is a great way to gauge the length of a feather wing.

What Is Dubbing Wax and Why Is It Important?

DUBBING WAX IS AN ESSENTIAL INGREDIENT FOR TYING the dubbed bodies on many important dry flies, nymphs, and wet flies. This extra-tacky wax comes in tubes. All fly shops stock it.

Dubbing wax is extremely easy to use. When you're ready to tie the body of the fly, swipe a small amount of wax on the thread. Next, spread a pinch of dubbing on the waxed section of thread; the wax makes the dubbing adhere to the fine thread. Spin the bobbin to tighten the dubbing around the thread like rope. Wrap the dubbed thread up the hook to make the body of the fly.

Here's an important tip: Keep the tube in your shirt pocket or close to your skin to keep the wax warm and soft. Softer wax is much easier to apply to the thread.

41

The Importance of Learning Thread Control

NOTHING IS MORE FRUSTRATING THAN HAVING THE thread snap at a critical moment when tying a fly: the thread unwraps, materials come loose, and the fly falls apart. Sometimes a small burr in the end of a metal bobbin tube nicks the fine fibers and weakens the thread, but I think some tiers leap to blaming their tools rather than examining their tying skills.

Mastering proper thread control is a basic fly-tying skill that is easy to master. Here's how.

Place a spool of thread in the bobbin, and mount a stout hook in the vise. Start the thread on the hook. Next, tightly grasp the spool of thread so no more thread can come out of the bobbin. Pull the bobbin until the thread snaps. Repeat this procedure several times until you have a feel for how much tension you can apply to the thread until it breaks. Repeat this exercise whenever you change thread diameters. You will quickly master thread control and rarely break thread when tying.

Tying a small, dry fly requires using very narrow thread. Learn the breaking strength of the thread you are using before tying the fly.

42

Are Natural Fly-Tying Materials Safe?

I NEVER THOUGHT I'D HEAR THIS QUESTION: "ARE MY FLY-tying materials safe to use?" But, several suppliers of fly-tying materials, especially the farmers who grow chickens for hackle, report receiving calls from concerned tiers asking about the safety of their natural materials—feathers and furs. Most of the concern arose from reports of the spread of avian flu. Rest assured that your fly-tying materials are completely safe to use.

The packaged materials you purchase at your local fly shop have all been carefully washed and preserved. This processing kills any bacteria that might have been on these products. They are entirely safe and disease-free.

Remember, however, that many of these materials contain dyes, and they certainly contain residue from the tanning process. When using natural materials, keep your fingers away from your mouth and eyes, and wash your hands to remove any chemical residue when you are done tying flies.

43

A Dash of Flash Can Improve a Fly

TIERS HAVE ADDED FLASH TO THEIR FLIES FOR CENTURIES. Traditionally, tinsel and wire were used to brighten patterns, but today we have many more options.

Almost all fly shops carry Krystal Flash and Flashabou, as well as many varieties of similar materials marketed under a host of different names. A few strands of one of these materials added to the wing of a streamer will brighten the fly and improve its ability to attract fish. And a small piece of Flashabou or similar material, pulled over the wing case of a nymph, will turn a decent fly into a real trout catcher. Some tiers use dubbing with flash to tie the bodies of dry flies; they swear that a bright floating pattern catches more fish than its dull-bodied cousin.

Flash materials are especially important to tying saltwater flies. A few strands of flash brighten a fly so a fish can see it from a greater distance, and the flash mimics the scales of a natural baitfish.

A few strands of flash material mimic the scales of a real baitfish.

Use Ultra Wire to Make Variations on Established Patterns

ULTRA WIRE, A PRODUCT OF WAPSI FLY, IS COPPER WIRE anodized in many colors. Ultra Wire is a fine material for making variations of established patterns and creating your own original flies.

Ultra Wire comes in four sizes, so you can use it to tie a wide variety of flies. It is durable, easy to use, and has become a favorite material for making fish-catching nymphs, wet flies, and streamers. Use regular copper or silver Ultra Wire as called for in your favorite fly pattern recipe, or use another color of Ultra Wire to make a neat variation of that pattern. Simple products such as Ultra Wire open new and exciting possibilities in our tying.

Red Ultra Wire jazzed up this simple modern-looking nymph pattern.

45

What Hairs and Furs Do I Need to Tie Flies?

THERE ARE DOZENS OF HAIRS AND FURS USED TO TIE FLIES, but you only need a few different varieties to start. You'll find everything you need at your local fly shop.

A patch of elk hair is essential for making the Elk-Hair Caddis, but fine deer hair is a perfectly acceptable substitute. Squirrel tail hair—gray and red fox squirrel—is ideal for making the wings on streamers. Bucktails, which come in natural and many dyed colors, are essential for making the wings and bellies on baitfish imitations.

You'll see a lot of patterns that call for hare's-ear dubbing for making the bodies on smaller nymphs and wet flies. Some tiers buy the masks (yes, the faces) of rabbits, and clip the fur from the skins. A better solution is to purchase packaged hare's-ear dubbing; it comes in natural and a rainbow of dyed colors.

Angora dubbing or a similar coarse hair is ideal if you wish to tie larger nymphs. Angora gives a fly a fuller body, and the thicker fibers create the impression of legs.

Remember that all of these hairs and furs come in a variety of dyed colors, increasing the possibilities for crafting great fish-catching flies.

Even deer hair comes in a rainbow of colors.

46

Clean Glue from the Hook Eye before Removing the Fly from the Vise

IT'S UNAVOIDABLE: YOU WILL GET SOME GLUE IN THE hook eye when finishing a fly. Even the most experienced tier occasionally gets a drop of cement in the hook eye. The seasoned fly dresser, however, knows to immediately remove the glue before popping the fly from the vise rather than trying to poke it out when fishing.

A bodkin needle is a handy tool for removing this glue. A better method, however, is to thread a small hackle or piece of peacock herl all the way through the hook eye. The soft, feather fibers neatly clean away the cement and leave the eye open for your tippet when fishing.

Spend your time on the water casting to the fish, not primping your flies!

Always clean the glue from the hook eye before placing a new pattern in your fly box. ▶

Accurate Thread Wraps Reduce Bulk

A BIG, BULBOUS THREAD HEAD OR THICK BUMPS IN THE body ruin the appearance of a finished fly. Typically, this common problem is due to using too many and needless wraps of thread. Further, making a few accurate and firm wraps creates a more durable fly than using a bunch of haphazard wraps.

Apply the material to the hook, and make one or two loose thread wraps. Check that the material is in the correct position. Next, slowly tighten the thread and simultaneously make a couple more firm wraps to lock the material in place. Follow this simple procedure every time you add a material.

With practice, you'll quickly use this simple technique when wrapping thread. Your flies will have a trimmer, more polished look, and they will be more durable and less apt to fall apart when fishing.

Learn how to make accurate thread wraps, and you'll soon be tying flies such as this classic salmon pattern.

48

Avoiding Unsightly Bumps in Fly Bodies

YOU WANT TO MAINTAIN THE SLENDER APPEARANCE IN fine fly bodies made with floss, thread, tinsel, and similar materials; small bumps will spoil the appearance of the finished flies.

The tag ends of the materials you tie to the hook should almost equal the length of the shank. The long tag ends will create a level underbody. And use size 8/0 (70 denier) or 6/0 (140 denier) flat-waxed thread. Spin the bobbin counterclockwise after every dozen wraps to remove any twist from the thread and keep the material lying flat and smooth on the hook.

1. Tie on the tinsel and red floss. Note that the tag ends of the material equal the length of the hook shank.

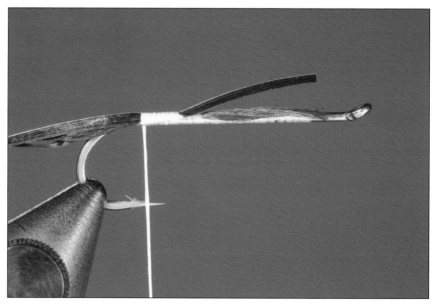

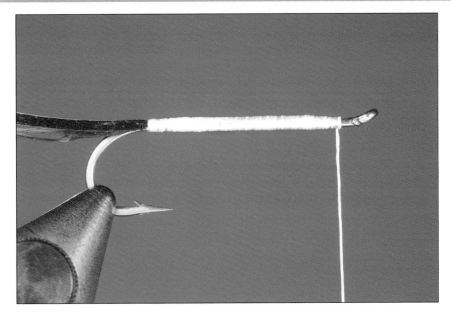

2. Wrap the thread up the hook. The tag ends under the thread create a level underbody.

3. Here is the completed body of the fly. The body is level and smooth.

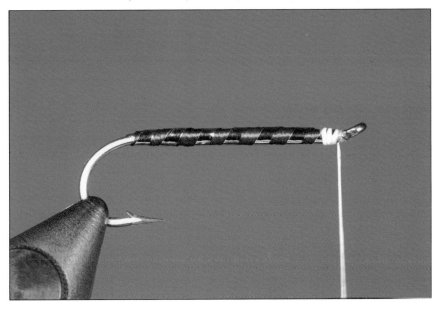

The Parts of a Hook

YOU PROBABLY ARE FAMILIAR WITH THE TERMS HOOK EYE and point; even if you are not, you could probably figure them out just by looking at a hook. There are, however, terms that describe many of the other parts of a hook as well.

Barb: The small, sharp tab of metal pointing in the opposite direction from the hook point. The barb prevents the hook from becoming accidentally disengaged from the flesh in the fish's mouth.

Bend: The bend is part of the hook that bends down and curves to the sharp end of the hook.

Eye: The ring at the front of the hook where you tie the fly to the leader when fishing. The eye can be straight, turned up, or turned down.

Gap: The distance between the hook point and the shank.

Point: This is the sharp business end of the hook.

Shank: The shank is the length of the hook from the eye to the beginning of the bend. The shank can be straight, but on some nymph hooks it is slightly curved.

Spear: The distance between the tip of the point and the tip of the barb.

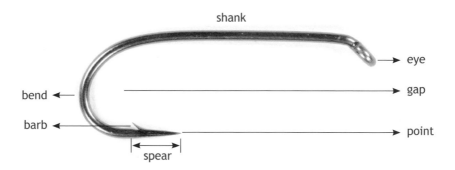

De-Barb the Hook before Tying the Fly

MANY ANGLERS USE BARBLESS HOOKS TO REDUCE DAMAGE to the mouths of the fish they catch, and to speed up releasing fish. While you can buy barbless hooks, most anglers simply crimp down the barbs on their flies. There is a chance, however, that smashing down the barb will weaken the hook and cause it to break; this problem is more common with fine dry-fly hooks than heavy-wire streamer or saltwater hooks. If you plan to fish barbless, bend down the barb before tying the fly. This way, if the hook does break, you've only wasted a hook, not your time and materials tying a fly.

The barb was mashed down on the hook before tying this fly.

51

Poppers Are Fun and Easy to Make

FLY FISHING FOR BASS AND PANFISH IS A HOOT, AND SO IS making poppers. If you plan to spend any time fishing for these easy-to-catch species, then you should also schedule some time to make a few poppers.

Small corks, which you can buy at almost any hardware store, are ideal for making popper bodies. In addition to the corks, you'll need hooks, size 3/0 thread, superglue, feathers, rubber legs, and a couple of bottles of hobby enamel paint. Simply wrap a layer of thread on the hook shank, and cut a shallow, narrow channel in the side of a cork. Coat the thread with superglue, and press the hook into the channel in the cork. Paint the body in your favorite colors, and tie feathers, rubber legs, and perhaps a few strands of flash material behind the body.

Many fly shops sell small kits containing popper bodies, hooks, and construction instructions. Be sure to follow the instructions for selecting the correct type of paint for the materials used to make the bodies.

Crafts Store Fun

WHILE WE ENCOURAGE YOU TO SUPPORT YOUR LOCAL FLY shop whenever possible, it's impossible to talk about modern fly tying and not mention the great materials found in crafts stores.

Your local crafts store, as well as the crafts section of a large discount retailer, is a treasure trove of ideas for creating scads of new fish-catching flies. Look for closed-cell foam, felts, paints, epoxies and glues, doll eyes, sparkle and flash materials, and so much more, and imagine all of the original patterns you will be able to create.

Making flies requires developing the proper tying skills and having a good imagination. Visit your local crafts store, let your imagination run wild, and develop your own new flies using unusual fly-tying materials.

Tying Dry Flies that Ride Higher and Float Longer

What Are the Parts of a Dry Fly?

WHILE THERE ARE A WIDE VARIETY OF DRY FLIES, MANY contain common parts. Most dry flies, especially the popular patterns, contain the following ingredients: a tail, body, wing, and hackle collar.

Body: A body is commonly made with fine dubbing, a hackle quill stripped of its fibers, thread or floss. A body might have a rib tied of fine wire or thread. The rib strengthens the body and creates a segmented appearance.

Hackle collar: The hackle collar is one of the most outstanding features of a dry fly. Wrap a feather plucked from a hackle cape around the hook shank to form the collar.

Tail: A tail is typically tied using the fibers from a hackle or other feather, or some fine hair.

Wing: Dry-fly wings are tied using fine hair such as calf tail, feather fibers, sections clipped from feathers, and whole feathers.

wing

body

tail

hackle collar

54

Three Common Dry-Fly Wings

READ FLY-TYING BOOKS AND MAGAZINE ARTICLES, AND you'll find a great many styles of dry-fly wings. When learning to tie flies, however, concentrate on making the three most common forms of wings.

Hair wings are made using elk hair, deer hair, or some other fine hair. Tie this style of wing flat along the top of the hook to simulate caddisfly or stonefly wings.

Upright wings are made using feather fibers, sections of fibers clipped from whole teal, wood duck, or mallard flank feathers, and the entire rounded tips of hen hackles or English partridge feathers. Tie these wings to the top of the hook to simulate mayfly wings.

Wing posts are used to tie parachute dry flies. A wing post is typically fine hair or polypropylene yarn, and a hackle is wrapped around the base of the wing post to complete the parachute.

Hair wing

Wing post

Upright wings using sections of feather

55

Prepare the Hackle before Tying the Fly

TAKE A FEW MOMENTS TO PREPARE A HACKLE BEFORE tying it to the hook. It takes just seconds, it will make wrapping the feather around the hook much easier, and the finished fly will look much better.

First, select the proper hackle to match the hook size. Typically, the length of the fibers should equal one and one-half to two times the width of the gap. This rule of thumb usually applies to both wet and dry flies.

Strip the excess fluffy fibers from the base of the hackle. Continue stripping fibers from the bottom one-quarter to one-third of the feather until you reach the thinnest part of the quill; this is called the "sweet spot" of the feather.

Next, strip a few more fibers from the side of the feather that will lay against the hook shank; this will allow the feather to wind neatly onto the hook.

Note the fibers brushed out perpendicular to the feather stem. Strip and discard these fibers, and use the remaining piece of hackle to tie the fly.

How to Wrap a Regular Dry-Fly Hackle

WRAPPING A HACKLE COLLAR FOR TYING A STANDARD DRY fly is one of the most important things you will learn. It is often best to practice wrapping hackle collars on a bare hook before attempting to tie a fly.

After preparing the hackle, start the thread on the hook. Tie the bare hackle stem to the hook with the dull, concave side of the feather facing you. (The concave side is the side of the feather that was against the skin of the hackle cape.)

Wrap the hackle after you have tied the wings. Grasp the tip of the feather with hackle pliers. Make one complete wrap of hackle behind the wings, then make one complete wrap directly in front of the wing. Now make three or four more close wraps of hackle; the quills should actually touch. Tie off and clip the excess hackle tip. Make a neat thread head, whip-finish the thread, and clip.

1. Tie the feather to the hook with the concave side facing you.

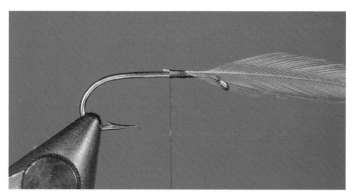

2. Grasp the tip of the feather with your hackle pliers (outside of the photo). Raise the feather and make one complete wrap around the hook.

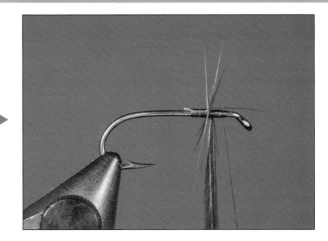

3. Continue wrapping the hackle up the hook.

4. Carefully catch and tie off the remaining piece of hackle. Cut off the excess hackle. Brush back the hackle fibers. Make three or four firm thread wraps to lock the hackle collar in place.

57

Judging Hackle Size

CHOOSING THE CORRECT SIZE OF HACKLE TO MAKE A DRY or wet fly is one of the challenges you will face as a new tier. You can buy presorted hackles packaged to tie flies in a limited range of sizes—for example, a package might contain feathers to tie size 16 and 14 flies—but you will eventually want to own full capes that offer the complete range of feather sizes. This will require you to judge the length of the hackle fibers to match the size of fly you are making.

A hackle gauge, which you'll find in your local fly shop, is a handy tool for measuring the size of a hackle. Simply bend the feather around the post in the base of the gauge to fan out the hackle fibers; this is similar to wrapping a hackle around a hook shank. Read the length of the fibers on the gauge.

Another option is to place a hook in your vise and fold the feather around the bottom of the hook as if you were going to wrap the hackle collar. The fibers will fan out so you can judge the length. If the fibers are too long or short, select another feather and repeat. Typically, the fibers should equal about one and one-half times the width of the hook gap, but you can adjust this dimension as you gain more experience as a tier and angler.

This hackle gauge, which fits onto the stem of a vise, is offered by Whiting Farms. ▶

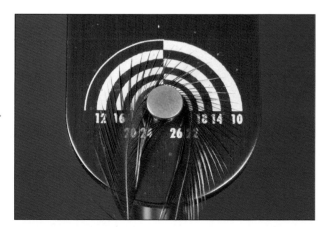

58

Dubbing for Dry Flies versus Wet Flies— What's the Difference?

DUBBING IS USED TO TIE THE BODIES OF TROUT FLIES. When making imitations of the most important adult insects—mayflies, caddisflies, and stoneflies—use dubbing that has fine fibers and twists easily on the thread. This material makes compact, slender bodies that best match the profiles of real insects.

Most modern dry-fly dubbing is some variety of synthetic material. Antron dubbing, which comes in a dizzying array of colors, is one of the most popular. Add a package of olive, tan, brown, and golden yellow dry-

Use fine dubbing when tying flies such as this Sulfur Compara-dun.

fly dubbing to your fly-tying kit, and you'll be set to make imitations of dozens of important adult insects.

Use coarser dubbing for making nymphs and wet flies. Once again, think of the real insects: a nymph or emerging insect usually has a broader body and dangling, kicking legs. A material containing thick, coarse fibers yields a thicker body and imitates the legs of the natural insect.

Rabbit dubbing is ideal for making the bodies on small nymphs and wet flies. The soft fur helps create a narrow body, and the guard hairs mimic the legs of the insect. Coarse, Angora goat dubbing remains a favorite material for tying larger stonefly and dragonfly nymph imitations. A small selection of colors—black, brown, dark olive, tan, and golden yellow—is all you'll need to tie most nymphs and wet flies.

What Is Cul de Canard?

CUL DE CANARD FEATHERS, WHICH COME FROM THE RUMP of a duck near the preen gland, have become one the most important ingredients for tying high-floating dry flies. You'll want to add cul de canard to your collection of fly-tying materials as soon as possible.

Some tiers believe that cul de canard, which comes in many natural and dyed colors, contains oils that keep these feathers afloat, but this is not so: One of the first steps in the dyeing process is to remove most of the natural oils so the dyes will adhere to the material. Yet, dyed cul de canard still floats like a cork. How can this be? Because the fibers on a cul de canard feather have microscopic hooks that trap air bubbles and keep the feather (and the duck) afloat; one cul de canard feather contains thousands of these tiny hooks.

Use cul de canard to make the wings on dry flies. Develop your own unsinkable flies, or add cul de canard to established patterns: a single cul de canard plume, placed under the wing of an Elk-Hair Caddis, increases the buoyancy of this time-tested fly.

The tier used gray cul de canard to make the wing on this emerger imitation. ▶

How to Make a Parachute Wing Post

TO TIE PARACHUTE-HACKLED DRY FLIES, YOU'LL FIRST need to know how to tie the proper wing post.

You may make the wing post using several common materials, including closed-cell foam and fine hair. Polypropylene yarn, which comes in a variety of realistic and bright colors, is one of the easiest ingredients to use. Many tiers select white, fluorescent pink, or fluorescent orange because these wings are easy to spot on the water; use one of these colors if you plan to fish in poor light or if you're having difficulty seeing your flies on the water.

In addition to the wide selection of colors, polypropylene yarn adds little bulk to a fly and requires only a few well-placed thread wraps to lock in place. Polypropylene wing posts are particularly useful when dressing small flies.

1. Fold a small section of yarn under the hook. Lock the yarn in place using three of four figure-eight wraps crossing on the bottom of the hook.

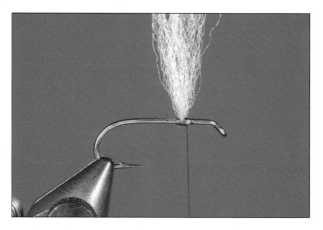

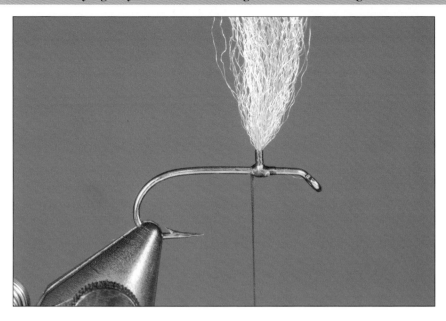

2. Wrap the thread up the base of the wing post. We'll complete tying the fly in the next tip.

61

How to Wrap a Parachute Hackle

TYING A PARACHUTE HACKLE MAY SEEM LIKE AN ADVANCED fly-tying technique, but it really isn't complicated. The key is to break the task down into several steps.

First, wrap a small thread base around the base of the wing (see Tip No. 60.) Next tie the hackle to the base of the wing. Before wrapping the feather, tie the body of the fly. Finally, wrap the parachute hackle.

Think of these tasks as small individual steps, and you will quickly learn how to make fine parachute hackle dry flies.

1. Tie the hackle to the base of the wing post. Wrap the thread to the end of the hook shank.

2. Tie on several hackle fibers to form the tail of the fly.

3. Spin a pinch of fine dubbing on the thread and wrap the body of the fly.

4. Wrap the hackle down the wing post to form the parachute hackle collar. Carefully tie off the hackle behind the hook eye, and clip the surplus. Wrap a neat thread and tie off the thread; It's okay to brush back the hackle fibers and wing if you need room to work. Snip the thread.

How to Tie Split Upright Wings

MANY OF OUR MOST FAMOUS DRY FLIES ARE TIED WITH two split, upright wings: the Royal Wulff, the Quill Gordon, the Light and Dark Hendricksons, and many others. Some of these wings are tied using fine hair such as calf tail (select the straightest you can find—nothing with a lot of curl), mallard flank feathers, lemon wood duck flank feathers, and mallard flank feathers dyed to imitate wood duck.

The trick is not to tie on two separate wings, but to tie on a single clump of material—hair or feather fibers—and then divide the wings into two. If necessary, place careful thread wraps around the base of each wing to hold it in place. When learning to make this style of wings, it helps to start tying a slightly larger fly to get a feel for working with the material and crafting the wings. For example, if you wish to tie a batch of size 14 Light Hendricksons for the early May hatch on a local trout stream, start by making a size 10 or 12 fly, then tackle the smaller pattern.

Let's see how to tie a pair of classic upright and divided wings using a wood duck flank feather.

1. Tie the feather to the top of the hook; the tips of the fibers, which will form the wings, are about equal to the length of the hook shank.

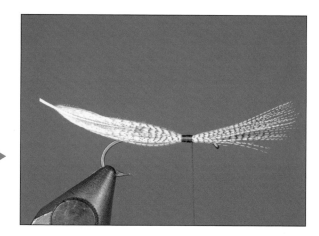

2. Hold the clump of fibers upright. Fold and pinch the base of the fibers back. Wrap a tiny dam of thread in front of the clump to hold the fibers up.

3. Split the clump in two. Make a series of figure-eight wraps between the fibers to create the two wings.

63

How to Tie a Wulff Hackle Collar

TO TIE THE ROYAL WULFF AND SIMILAR HIGH-FLOATING dry flies, you'll need to learn one of two primary ways to create the trademark bushy hackle collars.

First, you can use an extra-long, dry-fly saddle hackle. One of these feathers, which sometimes measure up to ten inches long, is sufficient to tie collars on either three or four regular dry flies or one or two Wulff patterns.

You may also use two or three normal cock hackles to make a single Wulff hackle collar. Wrap one hackle on the hook, then tie off and clip the surplus hackle tip. Wrap the second and then the third feathers to create a bushy Wulff hackle collar.

The key to both of these methods is to allow ample space on the hook shank to fashion the collar. Also, rocking the feathers back and forth while wrapping prevents each new wrap of hackle from binding down the fibers of previous wraps.

This unusual looking Royal Wulff has a very specific purpose; this heavily hackled and bushy fly is used to catch Atlantic salmon and steelhead. The fly makes a wake across the surface of the water and generates angry strikes from the fish.

Quills Make Great Dry-Fly Bodies

STRIPPED HACKLE QUILLS ARE A TRADITIONAL INGREDIENT for tying slender, tapered, segmented bodies on many dry and wet flies. The material is easy to use, and the finished bodies are very realistic looking.

The long feathers from the base of hackle capes are ideal for making stripped quills; they are rarely used for tying flies and are otherwise wasted. Pluck enough feathers for the flies you wish to tie. Strip the fibers from the hackles to reveal the bare quills. Place the quills in a dish of water to soften for tying; dry quills might crack and split when wrapping fly bodies. Next, tie the slender tip end of the quill to the end of the hook. Grasp

Mike Valla, a master at tying the classic Catskill dry flies, dressed this timeless Quill Gordon.

the fatter base of the quill with your hackle pliers, and wrap the body. Tie off and clip the excess quill, and complete the fly. You can leave the body in the natural color of the quill, or allow it to dry and then color it with a permanent marker. I also strengthen the quill body with a drop of cement.

Stripped peacock quills, which are pieces of peacock herl with the turquoise green fibers removed, are also used to tie the dainty bodies on classic dry flies. Sometimes you can find packages of stripped peacock quills in a fly shop, but you'll probably have to make your own. Simply draw a piece of herl between your forefinger and thumbnail; the nail will strip the fibers from the quill. You can also remove the fibers using a pencil eraser.

Mike Valla tied this perfect Cahill Quill dry fly.

Big Ideas for Tying
Tiny Flies

SOMETIMES TROUT ARE FEEDING ON SMALL INSECTS; you'll see them sipping the bugs from the surface of the water. You'll have to match the hatch with an imitation of the same size; without a diminutive dry fly or emerger, you will not catch fish. Tying small flies—sizes 20 and smaller—is consequently another fly-tying skill you will want to learn.

Use a vise that has jaws that can accommodate small hooks and leave ample room for you to tie the fly; If you are in the market for a vise, buy one that will allow you to tie flies of all sizes. Fine-tipped scissors are also essential for tying small flies; with them, you will be able to slip the scissor tips in and carefully snip excess materials from the hook. Thin-diameter thread such as size 8/0 (70 denier) is another mandatory item for tying tiny flies. There is also gossamer gel-spun thread, size 50 denier, which is very narrow yet extremely strong. And, you might wish to use some sort of magnifying device—a gooseneck magnifier or even low-power reading glasses—to better see your work.

66

Spinners Are Critical to Consistent Fishing Success

MANY NEW ANGLERS AND FLY TIERS OVERLOOK THE importance of spinners to consistent fly-fishing success. A spinner is an adult mayfly that has returned to the river or lake to mate, with the females laying their eggs. After mating, the exhausted insects lie on the surface of the water with their wings outstretched. Looking like small crosses, the spinners are easy targets for trout that want to gorge themselves. When the trout exhibit this feeding behavior, no fly other than a spinner imitation will catch a fish. I have experienced this on Vermont's Battenkill River, Colorado's North Platte, and even in remote waters in Labrador.

There are many spinner patterns, but the easiest solution to creating a good imitation is to tie a regular dry-fly tail and body. Next, tie a few strands of white or light-gray polypropylene yarn across the top of the hook to form the wings of a spent spinner. Spin a tiny pinch of dubbing on the thread and wrap the thorax of the fly.

Whenever you tie a few dry flies to match the mayfly hatches on your local waters, be sure to twist up a few spinners. On your next fishing trip, you'll be prepared to match the beginning as well as the end of the hatch, and you'll continue catching fish throughout the day.

Sometimes using a spinner imitation, such as this Rusty Spinner, is the key ▶ to fishing success. Be sure to make a few spinners whenever you tie dry flies.

67

Foam Flies Float Forever

CLOSED-CELL FOAM HAS BECOME A FAVORITE MATERIAL for tying dry flies. It is tough, comes in many colors, and is unsinkable. You can buy sheets of foam in several useful thicknesses for making the bodies of flies, and narrow cords of foam for making wing posts. Some tiers use foam to create outlandish-looking grasshoppers, crickets, and similar patterns, and others incorporate foam into more realistic looking flies.

Foam flies are especially useful as part of a dry fly-dropper rig. Use the foam fly as a high-floating strike indicator. Attach a short piece of tippet material to the bend in the fly's hook, and tie a small nymph or emerger to the other end of the tippet.

When tying with foam, take care not to cut into the material with the thread. Hold the material in position, and make two or three gentle thread wraps. Gradually tighten the thread and make two or thread more wraps. If necessary, add a small drop of superglue to the thread wraps to lock the foam to the hook.

This foam-bodied salmonfly imitation is unsinkable! ▶

68

Tie Off—Don't Clip— the Excess Hackle Tip

FLY-TYING GURU AL BEATTY SAYS IT IS BETTER TO TIE OFF— not clip—the excess hackle tip after wrapping the collar of the fly. He uses this simple method to create good-looking, fish-catching patterns.

Tie the fly and wrap the hackle following the regular methods. Carefully tie off the excess hackle tip using three wraps of thread. Next, lift the hackle tip, and wrap the thread between the hook eye and the surplus tip. Fold the tip up into the hackle collar. Wrap the thread back over the base of the tip; the tip becomes hidden in the full hackle collar. Wrap a neat thread head, and tie off and clip the thread.

This method of tying off the excess hackle tip is quick and easy, and prevents small fibers from clogging the hook eye and making it difficult to tie the fly to the leader while fishing.

1. First, wrap the hackle collar of the fly. Wrap the collar almost to the hook eye. Do not tie off and clip the excess hackle tip yet.

2. Tie off the hackle tip on top of the hook. Brush back the hackle fibers and surplus piece of feather. Wrap the thread toward the end of the hook; wrap over the hackle tip and the base of the first few fibers.

3. Clip the excess hackle near the thread head; any remaining piece of feather blends into the collar.

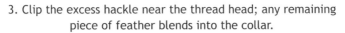

Tie Visible Dry Flies

POOR EYESIGHT, FOAM AND FROTH IN THE WATER, AND low-light conditions can make it difficult to see your fly on the surface of the water. But it is easy to tie flies that you'll be able to spot on the water a country mile away.

Tie the wings of the fly using brightly-colored, feather fibers or polypropylene yarn. Fluorescent orange, yellow, and chartreuse are favorite colors for making flies more visible. Use the identical tying techniques you would use when tying a regular pattern. And don't worry: There is no evidence to suggest that these brightly colored wings spook even the wariest fish.

Keep an eye on your fly: give it a colorful wing so you can see it on the water under all fishing conditions.

A bright yarn wing post makes it easy to spot this fly on the water.

What Is a Terrestrial, and Why Should I Care?

MANY OF THE FLIES WE TIE ARE DESIGNED TO IMITATE aquatic insects: stoneflies, mayflies, caddisflies, damselflies, dragonflies, and more. Aquatic insects live their immature lives in the water, and eventually emerge to mate. The females then drop their eggs into the water to repeat the lifecycle.

If you live in grasshopper country, be sure to tie a few 'hopper' imitations for mid-summer fishing.

Terrestrial insects are born and live exclusively on dry land: grasshoppers, ants, crickets, beetles, inchworms, and anything else that can fall into the water and become a meal for the fish. During mid to late summer, terrestrial patterns can spell the difference between having a good or a great day on the stream.

Wherever you fly fish for trout, terrestrials will catch fish. In fact, many anglers travel to Montana in August to cast grasshopper imitations into that state's rivers, and cricket patterns have an important place on Pennsylvania's storied limestone streams. As a tier, you will want to learn to make some patterns to match these important insects.

Tying Nymphs and Emergers that Catch More Trout

What Are the Parts of a Nymph?

NYMPHS ARE CRITICAL TO TROUT-FISHING SUCCESS, AND you'll want to learn how to make a variety of these important patterns. First, we need to review the basic parts of a common nymph imitation. A basic nymph contains a tail, abdomen, thorax, wing case, and legs.

Abdomen: This is the first section of the body. Although the entire body is sometimes fashioned with the same material, the abdomen is usually quite distinct from the front of the body. Natural and synthetic dubbings are the most common materials for tying the abdomen. An abdomen often has a rib made of wire to increase the strength of the fly and create a segmented appearance.

Legs: Almost all nymph imitations have some sort of legs. On smaller patterns, such as the Hare's-Ear Nymph, the coarse guard hairs in the rabbit dubbing used to tie the thorax are sufficient to suggest legs. You can also use feather fibers or strands of rubber to make legs on nymphs.

Tail: The tail and antennae are commonly tied with feather fibers, fur, or rubber legs. A tail made using a small tuft of soft rabbit fur flows in the water and makes a nymph look as if it is swimming and struggling in the current. Only larger stonefly nymph imitations typically have antennae.

Thorax: The thorax is the front half on the body. The thorax is typically thicker than the abdomen to create the proper silhouette. A slightly coarse variety of dubbing is ideal for making a nymph thorax. A thorax usually does not have a rib.

Wing case: This is the back of the thorax. The wing case is sometimes referred to as the *wing pads*.

Rubber Legs, Tails, and Antennae for Nymphs

YOU CAN USE MANY NATURAL MATERIALS TO TIE THE TAILS, legs, and antennae on nymphs; hackle fibers, biots, and some stiff hairs are popular ingredients. Rubber legs, however, make some of the best append-ages. This inexpensive material comes in several thicknesses and colors, and it is extremely easy to use. All you have to do is fold a piece of rubber legs around the thread and tie it to the end of the fly to make the tails. Repeat this to tie a set of legs to each side of the fly, and repeat this again to tie antennae on the front of the fly.

My first choice is to use rubber legs when tying nymphs. The material is indestructible when tying and fishing.

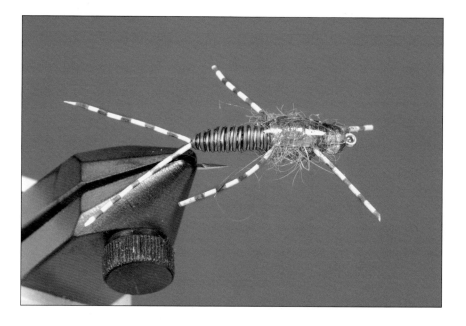

Do You Need to Tie Realistic Looking Flies?

EVERYONE WANTS TO LEARN HOW TO TIE FLIES THAT LOOK like real insects, but simpler generic patterns probably catch more fish. The competitors in the World Fly-Fishing Championships have learned that it is better to use flies that suggest the appearance of a variety of insects than it is to mimic specific species of bugs. These expert anglers argue that the general size, shape, and color of a pattern is far more important than if it bristles with realistic-looking tails, legs, and whiskers. Now we know why the time-honored Hare's-Ear and Pheasant-Tail Nymphs—which can imitate a large number of insects anywhere in the world—remain so popular.

It's easy to get overwhelmed with the huge number of patterns found in books, magazines, and online. To avoid confusion, learn to tie a handful of flies that match a cross section of the most common nymphs you find clinging to the rocks in your home waters.

The realistic looking nymph on the left is great, but the two simpler flies on the right will probably catch more fish.

Pheasant-Tail Fibers Make Realistic Looking Nymph Bodies

WITH TIME, YOU WILL LEARN HOW TO USE DUBBING TO make the bodies on nymphs and wet flies. If you're still fumbling with this technique, however, spend an evening making flies using pheasant-tail fibers.

All fly shops sell pheasant-tail feathers. When wrapped on a hook shank, the fibers make wonderfully segmented and mottled bodies. The famous Pheasant-Tail Nymph is made almost entirely from the fibers of a pheasant-

Pheasant-tail fibers were used to tie the tail and abdomen on this nymph imitation.

tail feather; this pattern, which was first created more than 100 years ago, is still used around the world to catch trout.

You can also use pheasant-tail fibers to make a realistic looking caddisfly case. This easy-to-tie pattern, which is an excellent imitation of the common *Hydrosphyce* larva found in many rivers, is simply pheasant fibers for the body and chartreuse tying thread for the head. How simple is that?

So, if you're still struggling to use dubbing, make some flies using pheasant-tail fibers, go to your local stream, and catch some fish!

Tricks for Stronger Wing Cases

MANY NYMPH PATTERNS CALL FOR WING CASES MADE OF slips clipped from turkey or pheasant-tail feathers. These flies are great for catching trout, but the wing cases are a little fragile and the teeth of fish quickly tear them up.

A drop of cement on top of the wing case toughens this part of the fly; a drop of epoxy makes it indestructible. If you prefer the duller appearance of the natural material, place the drop of glue on the inside of the piece of feather before folding it over the top of the fly to create the wing case.

Another option is to replace the piece of feather with a narrow strip of mottled-colored Thin Skin. This vinyl material comes in a wide variety of colors, including imitations of turkey and pheasant feathers. It's a great substitute for real turkey and pheasant.

A drop of epoxy on the wing case made this pattern almost bulletproof.

Flashy Dubbing Improves Nymphs and Wet Flies

ONCE UPON A TIME, ALL WE HAD WERE PLAIN DUBBINGS: rabbit, beaver, angora, and a host of other natural furs. You'll still find all of these materials in the fly-tying section of any well-stocked fly shop; they are required ingredients for making many of our most important patterns.

Today, however, we can also select from a host of new flashy dubbing materials. Some of these dubbings are blends of natural furs containing pinches of fine-fibered synthetic flash materials; a dash of flash can transform

The body on this simple larva imitation was made using a blended flash dubbing.

an ordinary fly into a real fish-catcher. Other products are 100 percent synthetic dubbing.

While some manufacturers add flash fibers to brighten plain, old-fashioned dubbing, there is also a practical reason for creating blended dubbing: Most synthetic dubbing is hard to apply to thread to wrap a neat body. With blended dubbing, the natural fur acts as a binder; it readily adheres to the tacky wax applied to the thread before adding the dubbing.

Unless you have a specific reason for using pure synthetic dubbing, blended dubbing is actually easier to use.

Do the Twist With Peacock Herl

MANY FAVORITE PATTERNS REQUIRE PEACOCK HERL FOR parts of the bodies. These metallic-green feather fibers, which come from the tail feathers of a peacock, make lovely flies, but the material is fragile and can quickly break when fishing. Twisting the herl around a piece of thread, like twisting the strands in a piece of string, strengthens the material and makes for a more durable fly. Let's see how to tie a strong peacock herl body on a simple wet fly.

When starting the thread on the hook, do not clip the tag end; leave it hanging off the back of the fly. Next, tie on the hackle. Wrap the thread to the end of the hook and tie on two pieces of peacock herl and a piece of wire; we'll eventually use the wire to make the rib of the fly. Twist the herl around the thread tag, and wrap the body of the fly.

We'll complete this wet fly in the next tip.

1. Start the thread and leave the tag end of the thread hanging off the rear of the hook. Tie on the hackle. Tie on the peacock herl and a piece of wire.

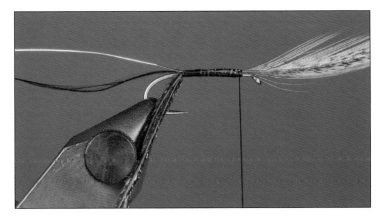

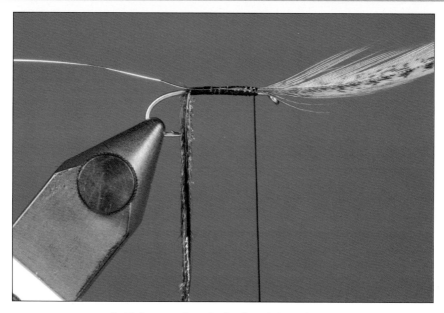

2. Twist together the herl and thread tag.

3. Wrap the body of the fly. Tie off and clip the excess herl and thread tag.
We'll finish the fly in the next tip.

A Counter-Wrapped Rib Strengthens a Fly Body

A RIB OF WIRE OR NARROW TINSEL GIVES A FLY A REALIStic segmented appearance and a dash of fish-attracting flash. When applied properly, the rib will also strengthen a body made of floss, thread, or peacock herl.

The trick is to counter-wrap the rib over the body; in other words, wrap the rib in the opposite direction from which you wrapped the body. Although the teeth of a fish might nick the body, the counter-wrapped rib prevents it from falling apart. This simple precaution will save your favorite flies—nymphs, wet flies, dry flies, and streamers—from hard use.

Let's complete the fly we started tying in the previous tip.

1. Counter-wrap the wire rib over the body. Tie off and cut the surplus wire.

2. Carefully wrap the hackle to form a sparse collar; the fibers suggest the legs of an emerging nymph. Tie off and clip the excess hackle.

Glass Beads Brighten Flies and Catch More Trout

PAT DORSEY IS ONE OF COLORADO'S BEST GUIDES. AFTER many seasons fishing his local rivers, he has unique insights into what catches trout. As a guide, Pat has to get his clients into fly fishing; he carries flies that he knows will help them succeed.

Pat created what he calls his Mercury series of flies. These subsurface patterns feature small silver-lined, fly-tying glass beads that look like mercury in tiny thermometers. The beads brighten the heads of the flies and attract the attention of the fish. You can add these beads to medium-sized nymphs and even your smallest midge imitations. As a bonus, silver-lined beads comes in a variety of colors, not only clear.

Try this experiment: tie a few of your favorite wet flies and nymphs with and without these bright beads. Take them to your local river and see which flies catch more trout.

The Craziest Fly Ever?

FLY FISHING IS CONSTANTLY EVOLVING. SOMETIMES NEW flies are developed to match changing fishing tactics, and sometimes fishing methods develop to take advantage of new patterns. Wladyslaw Niebies's unique fly is sometimes called Vladi's Worm—other times it is called the Condom Worm. Yes, Wladyslaw, who is one of the world's leading competitive fly fishermen, makes this fly using a real latex condom.

First, Wladyslaw bends a streamer hook to shape. He then wraps lead wire to make an exaggerated hump at the end of the hook shank. Next, he ties on and wraps a condom up the hook to form the worm. (You can easily substitute with a fly-tying material called Scud Back.) How ingenious is that? The wire and hook shape force the fly to turn over in the water and not snag the streambed, and the finished pattern imitates an aquatic worm. Vladi's Condom Worm spawned the revolutionary methods called European nymph fishing.

What's the moral of this story? Never be afraid to experiment with your fishing or fly tying. Try developing new patterns and angling methods. Who knows: perhaps you'll come up with the next fly that will revolutionize fly fishing?

Different Styles of Nymph Hooks

WHEN I STARTED TYING FLIES, ALL TROUT-FLY HOOKS HAD straight shanks. There's nothing wrong with straight-shanked hooks, except that most insects have slightly curved bodies. When nymphs are dislodged from the streambed and float with the current—which is when they are most vulnerable to fish—they generally assume a tucked or curved posture. A fly tied on a curved-shank, heavy-wire hook imitates the appearance of a real insect.

There are many brands and varieties of curved-shank nymph hooks. Some shanks have gentle curves; these hooks come in the widest range of sizes. Other hooks, often called scud or emerger hooks, have sharper bends and come in smaller sizes; these hooks are great for making a wide variety of small mayfly and stonefly nymphs, as well as scuds and emergers.

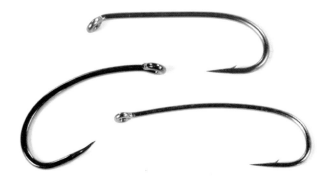

82

Simple Tips for Making Better Floss Bodies

SOME OF OUR MOST FAMOUS WET FLIES ARE TIED WITH floss bodies. Many years ago, tiers used real silk floss, but today you'll find spools of Rayon and other modern flosses in fly shops. Here are a couple of tricks to making perfect floss bodies.

There are two types of common floss: single strand and four strand. Four-strand floss is more difficult to use because you will have to separate and clip out an individual strand to tie each fly. Single-strand floss is a snap to use: just place the spool in a fly-tying bobbin, and tie the fly.

You'll place a clockwise twist in the floss as you wrap the material up the hook. Spin the bobbin counterclockwise after every ten wraps to remove this twist and keep the floss laying flat on the hook.

Finally, fold and tie down the tag end of the floss over the top of the fly. This will prevent the fine floss strands in the body or tag from slipping down the back of the hook when fishing the fly.

What Is a Soft-Hackle Wet Fly?

SOFT-HACKLE WET FLIES ARE SOME OF THE OLDEST PAT-terns. Primarily of English origins, they date back to at least the late fifteenth century. These patterns are sometimes referred to as soft hackles, and sometimes as wet flies; together—soft-hackle wet fly—the term is a perfect description of how they are tied, and how they are fished.

The key feature is a sparse, soft-fibered hackle that readily moves in the water and gives the fly the appearance of swimming as a real insect. The tail—if the fly has one—is generally tied very sparse, with feather fibers. The body is typically thread or floss, sometimes ribbed with tinsel. Other popular body materials are peacock herl and dubbing. Fish a wet fly under the surface to imitate a struggling nymph or emerging insect.

This classically inspired wet fly sports a modern bead head.

Many sparse soft-hackle wet flies are tied in dingy colors—brown, tan, and gray—similar to real insects; others are made with vibrant colors, especially bright floss bodies, tinsel ribs, and colorful feather wings.

Some classic wet flies have some of the most fanciful names: Greenwell's Glory, Parmacheene Belle, Bradshaw's Fancy, and Tup's Indispensable. And, before there was the Hare's-Ear Nymph, there was a simple wet fly called the Hare's Ear.

Make no mistake: These patterns have stood the test of time because they catch lots of fish!

What Are the Best Hackles for Tying Wet Flies?

FLY TIERS HAVE USED THE FEATHERS FROM MANY DIFFERent species of birds to make the hackles on wet flies: snipe, woodcock, grouse, English partridge, plover, starling, chicken, and more. Tiers simply used whatever birds—and feathers—were handy when creating their flies.

Today, due to regulations prohibiting the hunting of some species of birds, we have a more limited selection of feathers. But, we still have an ample variety of feathers from which to choose and can tie terrific softhackle wet flies.

Small hen hackles, in natural and dyed colors, are fine for tying wet flies. English partridge, which has always been an important ingredient for these patterns, is still widely available. And Coq de Leon, which is a Spanish variety of chicken now bred in the United States for its feathers, offers hackles that are a dead ringer for partridge. You'll find all of these feathers, and many others, at a well-stocked fly shop.

This buggy-looking wet fly was tied using a ginger-colored hen hackle. ▶

Wrapping the Hackle on a Wet Fly

A WELL-TIED, SOFT-HACKLE WET FLY HAS A VERY SPARSE hackle collar. Typically, the collar requires only one or two wraps of hackle. The goal is to add a few feather fibers to suggest the legs of a struggling nymph or emerger; an overly dressed fly will look unnatural.

There are two ways to wrap the collar. The first is simple: Tie the feather to the hook, make one or two wraps of hackle, and then tie off and clip the excess. This direct method produces a fine fly that will catch fish.

Some tiers prefer to make wet flies with hackle fibers that sweep more toward the rear of the fly. This requires folding the fibers in the same direction before wrapping the hackle. First, tie the hackle to the hook in the normal manner. Rub your thumbnail or the dull side of your scissors on the side of the feather you wish to fold. Lightly pinch the fibers together, and wrap the hackle once around the hook. Tie off and clip the surplus piece of feather. Folding the hackle is a slightly more advanced technique that yields a fine-looking wet fly.

1. We've tied on the hackle, the hackle-fiber tail, and a body using floss and peacock herl. Note that we tied on the hackle with the concave side facing us.

2. Make no more than two wraps of hackle; the fibers are supposed to suggest the legs of a nymph, so you don't want to overdress them. Tie off and clip the surplus piece of feather. Wrap a neat thread head, tie off, and snip.

How to Make a Dubbing Loop

MAKING A DUBBING LOOP IS A BASIC FLY-TYING TECHNIQUE; it is especially important for making nymphs and wet flies.

A dubbing loop is a simple way to apply dubbing—natural or synthetic fur—to a hook to create the body of the fly. First make a four- to five-inch-long loop of thread. Lightly smear dubbing wax onto the thread; this soft wax helps the dubbing adhere to the thread. Next, spread a pinch of dubbing in the loop. Spin the loop closed to form a miniature rope. Wrap the twisted loop up the hook to create the body of the fly.

Pay close attention to the proportions of dubbing you use when making a dubbing loop. Many tiers use too much dubbing, which results in a fat body. It requires only a pinch of dubbing to tie most flies. When in doubt about the amount of dubbing you are using, cut it in half; a slender fly typically looks better than an obese one.

We'll tie a complete wet fly in this tip. The thorax, which is rabbit dubbing, gives the fly a buggy appearance and prevents the soft-hackle fibers from collapsing against the hook when fishing.

1. Tie on the hackle, the tail, and a tinsel abdomen. Make a four-inch-long loop of thread. Wrap the working thread (coming out of the bobbin) at the base of the loop; these wraps lock the loop in place. Next, wrap the thread to the base of the hackle.

2. Lightly smear dubbing wax on the thread loop. Insert and spread a pinch of dubbing in the loop. Twist the loop closed.

3. Wrap the loop and dubbing on the hook to create the thorax of the fly. Tie off and clip the excess dubbing loop.

4. Wrap a sparse hackle collar. Tie off the surplus feather tip and complete the thread head.

87

The Pinch Wrap for Making Wet-Fly Wings

MANY WET FLIES HAVE WINGS. THE WINGS ARE OFTEN SLIPS clipped from matching turkey or goose wing quills. You'll find matched sets of feathers in almost any fly shop.

Clip a narrow slip from each feather. Place the slips together with the tip edges even. Grasp the slips between the thumb and forefinger of your non-tying hand, with the butt ends showing. Next, place the slips on top of the hook exactly where you wish to tie the wings. Pinch the wings and hook shank between your fingers, and make one loose wrap of thread on the base of the wings. Slowly tighten the thread and make two or three more wraps. Remove your fingers to check the position of the wings. If necessary, lightly adjust the slips until the wings are in the correct position. If you're still not pleased with the appearance of the fly, unwrap the thread and try again.

1. Clip slips from a matching set of duck quills.

2. Place the wings back to back with the tips even. Slip the wings onto the top of the hook. Pinch the wings to the hook and make two light wraps of thread. Continue pinching the wings in place, and slowly tighten the thread by pulling down on the bobbin.

3. Remove your fingers and examine the wings. If you are not entirely pleased with the results, you can rock the wings into position, and sometimes you will have to completely remove the wings and try again.

4. Carefully clip the butt ends of the wings; two or three small cuts typically work better than one complete cut.

Hotspots Catch More Fish

ADDING HOTSPOTS TO NYMPHS AND LARVAE PATTERNS IS one of the newest innovations in fly fishing. This is another lesson we are learning from the competitors to the World Fly-Fishing Championships.

Experienced anglers are discovering that a bright pinch of dubbing in the body, a band of bright thread or floss, or even a bright red or orange bead, can increase the ability of a fly to catch fish. This speck of color, which we call a hotspot, seems to attract the attention of the fish. The shape of the fly, as well as the proper presentation, then get the fish to strike.

The pinch of pink dubbing in the body adds to the fish attracting appeal of this simple caddis larva imitation.

Making Meaty Streamers for Catching Trophy Fish

What Is a Streamer?

A STREAMER IS USUALLY A FLY DESIGNED TO IMITATE A BAIT-fish. If it is true that big fish eat little fish, you'll typically catch larger fish using streamers. Streamers are important when fishing for large trout, and if you fish for bass, plan to tie a wide variety of streamers. Streamers are also important to success when fishing for saltwater species, especially striped bass, bluefish, false albacore, bonito, snook, and tarpon. Streamers were some of the first flies ever tied, and they remain a staple of most fly-fishing kits.

Streamers are also the most commonly used flies to catch Atlantic salmon and steelhead. Salmon and steelhead flies, like the one in the accompanying photograph, are some of the most beautiful and complex ever created. Tiers spend many years perfecting their craft, and often use a dozen or more materials to tie a single fly.

What Is an Attractor Pattern?

SURE, ALL THE FLIES WE TIE ARE SUPPOSED TO ATTRACT and catch fish—no one wants to tie flies that scare fish away. But, did you know that there are actually two different classes of flies: imitations and attractors?

Some patterns are tied to imitate specific forms of fish food; these are called *imitations*. Other flies match no specific form of fish forage, yet under the right circumstances they do an admirable job of attracting and catching fish; these patterns are called *attractors*. Although there are all sorts of attractor flies—dry flies, nymphs, and wet flies—streamers have always been used for catching most species of gamefish. And, when salmon and steelhead enter rivers to spawn and are no longer actively feeding, brightly-colored-attractor streamers are popular for catching these gamefish.

A fish attacks an attractor pattern out a sense of curiosity, territoriality, or anger.

Do You Need Special Tools to Tie Saltwater Flies?

GENERALLY SPEAKING, YOU WILL NEED NO SPECIAL TOOLS for tying the majority of saltwater patterns. The vise, bobbin, and scissors you use for making trout flies and bass bugs will suffice for tying saltwater flies. If, however, you plan to specialize in dressing saltwater flies, you might wish to consider selecting tools better designed for holding larger hooks and cutting hard synthetic hairs.

The Apte Tarpon fly is one of our most famous patterns; it was even depicted on a United States postage stamp.

It seems counterintuitive, but it's actually harder to get a vise to grasp a large saltwater hook; some vises must apply considerable force in order to hold the hook stationary. Some vises have small grooves machined in the jaws to grasp and hold larger hooks securely; these vises are ideal for tying everything from the tiniest trout to the largest saltwater flies.

Many saltwater flies require synthetic materials. These plastic and Mylar ingredients quickly dull ordinary scissors, so plan to include a set of scissors designed for cutting synthetic materials to your fly-tying kit.

And finally, if you make flies featuring epoxy, you'll want to add some sort of device that slowly turns the flies while the epoxy hardens.

Should I Use More Synthetic Materials to Tie Saltwater Flies?

MANY SALTWATER FLIES ARE MADE WITH SYNTHETIC MATE-rials. Plastic hairs, synthetic yarns, and large dumbbell eyes are common features on contemporary saltwater patterns. However, almost all of the classic saltwater flies are tied using common natural ingredients such as hackles and animal hair.

Make Lefty's Deceivers, Clouser Minnows, Bend Backs, and Whistlers using ordinary feathers, bucktail, tinsel, and thread. You can add a few strands of Flashabou or Krystal Flash to these flies if you like, but all of the other ingredients come from natural sources. And these flies still catch fish!

Study the latest fly-tying books and magazine articles, however, and you will see many patterns tied using only synthetic ingredients. These flies also catch their share of fish.

Synthetic or natural materials? The choice is yours.

This saltwater fly was tied using only synthetic ingredients.

93

Translucent Streamers Imitate Real Baitfish

SMALL BAITFISH SUCH AS MINNOWS AND DACE, AS WELL AS immature trout, bass, or other gamefish species, are all somewhat translucent, making that a key feature to include when tying their imitations. The best streamers, which often mimic baitfish, have a natural, translucent quality. Streamer wings tied with bucktail are also translucent. In fact, bucktail and marabou (which consists of soft, billowy feathers, usually from domestic turkeys) are both great natural materials for tying translucent wings that look alive in the water. If you prefer using synthetic fly-tying materials, use only small bunches of hair—Fishair, craft fur, or whatever—to create translucent wings that mimic the profiles of baitfish.

A good baitfish pattern matches the streamlined shape and translucence of a real fish.

Bucktail and hackles create streamers that appear slightly translucent in the water.

94

Superglue Welds, Dumbbells, and Bead-Chain to Flies

WHETHER YOU WISH TO TIE FLIES TO CATCH TROUT, BASS, or saltwater fish, you will want to add a few Clouser Minnows to your fly box. Many other subsurface patterns also feature bead-chain eyes. The trick to these patterns is securing the dumbbell and bead-chain eyes so they do not roll around the hooks. A drop of superglue will weld these parts in place and reduce the chance that they will move.

First, wrap a layer of thread on the hook where you plan to tie on the dumbbell or bead-chain eyes. Tie on the eyes using a series of firm figure eight wraps. Make three firm wraps between the eyes and the hook shank; these wraps should tighten the figure-eight wraps and cinch the eyes to the hook. Place a small drop of superglue on the thread wraps in the middle of the dumbbell or bead-chain, and make another series of firm figure-eight wraps. The fresh glue will penetrate all the thread wraps and lock the eyes in place.

A drop of super glue applied to the tight figure-eight wraps prevents the dumbbell from turning on the hook. Tying on the dumbbell is usually the first step in tying the fly.

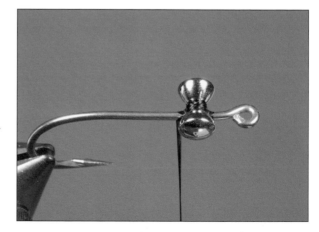

95

Selecting Bucktail for Streamers

ALL FLY SHOPS CARRY BUCKTAILS. A BUCKTAIL IS JUST what it sounds like: the tail of a deer. This universal fly-tying material comes in natural and a wide variety of dyed colors. Bucktail hair is one of the most commonly used materials for tying freshwater streamers and many saltwater patterns; a streamer that has wings tied using only bucktail hair is simply called a "bucktail."

It's temping to buy the largest bucktail hanging on the pegboard wall in your local fly shop, but that might be a mistake; although it contains the most hair and seems the more economical choice, the hairs might be poor for tying good flies. Many bucktails have crinkled hair, but a good one for tying streamers has straight hair. The flies tied using this material will have a sleeker, more streamlined appearance that simulates the profiles of a real baitfish. In addition to having fairly straight hair, a prime bucktail will have few broken strands.

A. K. Best is a fly-tying legend who lives in Colorado. This is his version of a Blacknose Dace sporting a bucktail wing.

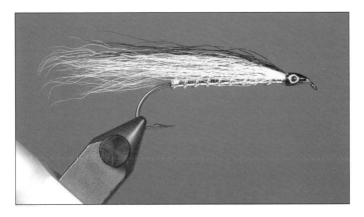

96

Selecting Saddle Hackle for Tying Streamers

SADDLE HACKLE IS COMMONLY USED TO TIE THE WINGS and tails on streamers and saltwater flies. Saddle hackles are the long feathers that hang down the sides of the back of a chicken, similar to a saddle draped over the back of a horse. Saddle hackle comes in natural as well as a wide assortment of dyed colors.

There are two ways to purchase hackle. Your local fly shop will carry entire pelts of saddle hackle, as well as individual packages of feathers. Avoid extremely long and skinny saddle hackle; these feathers come from chickens bred for dry-fly hackle and yield flies that look like swimming pencils. When tying streamers, select saddle hackles that have a fuller appearance and slightly rounded tip ends; these create flies that better match the silhouette of a baitfish

The author did the honors in tying this classic Gray Ghost. He selected feathers with full, rounded ends for the wings.

What Threads Should I Use to Tie Streamers and Saltwater Flies?

WHITE, BLACK, GRAY, AND RED ARE THE MOST POPULAR colors of thread for tying freshwater streamers and saltwater flies. And be sure to use white thread under any light-colored body materials such as floss; when the fly is wet, a darker color under the body will bleed through and spoil the appearance of the fly.

Select size 3/0 (210 denier) thread for tying most saltwater baitfish imitations and large streamers. Size 6/0 (140 denier) is fine for making small saltwater flies and most freshwater streamers.

Fine, clear monofilament thread is also popular for tying many saltwater flies and some streamers. This thread is very strong, and the transparent thread head you tie to complete a fly will allow the underlying materials to show through and match the color of a baitfish from the tip of its nose to the end of its tail.

Choosing Marabou for Streamers

MARABOU COMES FROM THE FEATHERS FOUND UNDER the wings of birds. These soft, billowy feathers give flies great swimming action when wet. Many knowledgeable fly tiers say marabou is one of their favorite materials for making streamers.

Marabou originally came from the marabou stork. Today, due to sound conservation regulations, taking a stork for any reason is no longer permitted. Nowadays, all fly shops sell marabou that comes primarily from domestic turkeys and chickens. Packages of marabou are widely available in white and many dyed colors. But all marabou is not created equal for tying.

Select marabou with thin stems and long, fluffy fibers.

Chicken marabou is fine for tying tails and other parts on nymphs and small flies, but you'll need something larger to tie the tails on Woolly Buggers and the wings on Marabou Muddler Minnows.

Use a sharp eye when selecting a package of marabou for tying streamers. Avoid marabou with thick stems that reach far up the feather. Instead, select a package with full, fluffy feathers and thin stems.

Although a popular fly-tying ingredient, marabou is not easy to tie to the hook; the soft fibers have a tendency to twist around the shank when tightening the thread. Lightly moisten the feather when tying the marabou to the fly. And measure the length of the wing or tail before tying on the feather. Adjust the feather until you are pleased with the appearance of the fly, and then tighten the thread. Clip away the excess butt end of the feathers; never cut the tip end.

What Hooks Should I Use to Tie Streamers And Saltwater Flies?

FOR TYING FRESHWATER STREAMERS DESIGNED TO IMI-tate real baitfish, select heavy-wire, long-shank hooks. Many of these hooks are designated as 4X and 6X long, but there are also 8X-long hooks that can easily measure three inches long. Most tiers prefer using 4X- and 6X- long hooks because it takes less time to make the bodies of the flies, and some anglers complain that 8X-long hooks do not hold fish as well as slightly shorter hooks.

There are various types of hooks designed for tying saltwater flies. These hooks are designed not to corrode in salt water. Stainless-steel hooks are

Here we see three styles of streamer hooks (*from the top going clockwise*): freshwater streamer hooks, stainless-steel saltwater hooks, and salmon/ steelhead hooks.

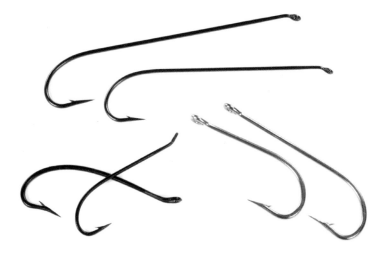

the most common variety; these come in a wide variety of sizes and lengths to make all styles of saltwater patterns. You'll also find hooks with various finishes that are designed not to corrode. Almost all of these hooks are excellent for tying flies, but you cannot sharpen the points if they become damaged. Sharpening a hook will require removing the finish and makes the point susceptible to rusting.

And finally, salmon and many steelhead flies are tied on hooks blackened with a procedure called *japanned*.

Making Shallow-Water Saltwater Flies Weedless

IF YOU PLAN TO TIE FLIES TO FISH THE FLATS FOR BONE-fish, redfish, and permit, you'll want to create patterns that do not catch grass and other vegetation. Sometimes, you'll even want the fly to rest on the bottom until a fish approaches, and then bring it alive with a stripping action; this also requires a pattern that will not snag.

Many of these flies, called flats patterns because they are commonly fished on sand and coral flats, have small dumbbells tied on the tops of the hooks. The dumbbells add weight to the top of the flies and cause them to flip over in the water so that the points are on top and cannot catch on the bottom. A small loop of heavy monofilament, tied on in front of the hook point, prevents the fly from catching grass and other debris.

This fine crab imitation sports both a small dumbbell and monofilament weed guard.

101

Adding a Monofilament Weed Guard to a Large Fly Is Easy

BRUSH, LOGS, MANGROVES, PILINGS, BOAT DOCKS, AND similar structures where fish hang out can claim flies—and lots of them! If you plan to fish such places, you'll want to add weed guards to your streamers and saltwater flies.

A monofilament weed guard is easy to tie. First, start the thread at the end of the hook shank. Wrap the thread halfway down the bend of the

A loop of monofilament prevents this squid imitation from catching weeds and other debris.

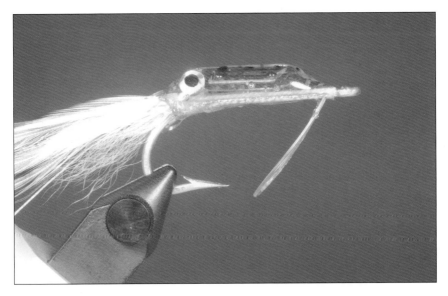

hook. Tie on the end of a two-inch-long piece of thirty-five-pound-test clear monofilament. Wrap the thread back up the bend, binding the end of the monofilament to the hook. Now tie the fly. Next, tie the other end of the monofilament behind the hook eye. The monofilament should loop slightly below the hook point to shield the point when the fly contacts objects in the water, yet it bends easily out of the way when a fish strikes.

A small piece of monofilament makes this saltwater pattern weedless.